Recent Research in Psychology

C.W. Stephan W.G. Stephan T.F. Pettigrew
Editors

The Future of Social Psychology

Springer-Verlag
New York Berlin Heidelberg London
Paris Tokyo Hong Kong Barcelona

Professor Cookie W. Stephan
Depts. of Sociology and Anthropology, New Mexico State University, Las Cruces, New Mexico 88003, USA

Professor Walter G. Stephan
Dept. of Psychology, New Mexico State University, Las Cruces, New Mexico 88003, USA

Professor Thomas F. Pettigrew
Stevenson College, University of California at Santa Cruz, Santa Cruz, California 95064, USA
and
Subfakulteit Psychologie, Vakgroep Sociale Psychologie, Universiteit van Amsterdam, Postbus 20218, 1000 HE Amsterdam, The Netherlands

Library of Congress Cataloging-in-Publication Data
The Future of social psychology : defining the relationship between sociology and psychology / Cookie White Stephan, Walter G. Stephan, Thomas F. Pettigrew, editors.
p. cm. — (Recent research in psychology)
Includes index.
1. Social psychology. I.Stephan, Cookie White. II. Stephan, Walter G. III. Pettigrew, Thomas F. IV. Series.
HM251.F89 1991
302—dc20 90-22480

Printed on acid-free paper.

Camera-ready copy provided by the editors.
Printed and bound by Edwards Brothers, Ann Arbor, Michigan.
Printed in the United States of America.

9 8 7 6 5 4 3 2 1

ISBN 0-387-97487-3 Springer-Verlag New York Berlin Heidelberg
ISBN 3-540-97487-3 Springer-Verlag Berlin Heidelberg New York

8 Bc/hg

Contents

Contributors

Carl W. Backman, Department of Sociology, University of Nevada, Reno, NV 89557, USA

James S. House, Department of Sociology and Institute for Social Research, University of Michigan, Ann Arbor, MI 48109, USA

Thomas F. Pettigrew, Stevenson College, University of California at Santa Cruz, Santa Cruz, CA 95064, USA and Subfakulteit Psychologie, Vakgroep Sociale Psychologie, Universiteit van Amsterdam, Postbus 20218, 1000 HE Amsterdam, The Netherlands

Carmi Schooler, Laboratory of Socio-Environmental Studies, National Institute of Mental Health, Federal Building, B1A-14, Bethesda, MD 20892, USA

Cookie White Stephan, Department of Sociology and Anthropology, New Mexico State University, Las Cruces, NM 88003, USA

Walter G. Stephan, Department of Psychology, New Mexico State University, Las Cruces, NM 88003, USA

Sheldon Stryker, Department of Sociology, Indiana University, Bloomington, IN 47405, USA

1
Introduction

Cookie White Stephan and Walter G. Stephan

This is a book about the two social psychologies--psychological social psychology and sociological social psychology--written by social psychologists from both disciplines. It focuses on the benefits and costs of interchange between psychological social psychology and sociological social psychology, with the ultimate goal of encouraging interaction among scholars in the two disciplines. The primary questions addressed are: What do the two disciplines have to offer each other? What are the barriers to fruitful interchange? How can these barriers be overcome?

In this introductory chapter we will first examine some historical reasons for the lack of interchange between the two social psychologies. Then we will provide a brief preview of the chapters to follow.

The Development of the Two Social Psychologies

The beginning of concern with the "social animal" can be traced to the ancient Greeks. However, social psychology's formal beginning is usually dated from Norman Triplett's 1897 publication of his findings on the effects of competition or from the publication in 1908 of two books including the words "Social Psychology" in their titles, one by the psychologist William McDougall and the other by the sociologist Edward Alsworth Ross. Thus, from its inception, social psychology was already divided into two distinct academic units, housed in the disciplines of sociology and psychology.

How did this process of division begin? Some 19th century ancestors of modern social psychology, such as Charles Darwin and William James, are central figures in the development of both sociological and psychological social psychology. However, during the 19th century significant differences in intellectual traditions began to emerge which led to differences between the two approaches to social psychology in the definitions, levels of analysis, methodologies, and theories they employed. We will briefly examine the distinctive intellectual heritages of the two social psychologies, and trace some of their consequences for the sociological and psychological social psychologies of today.

Sociological Heritage. The many 19th century intellectual precursors of modern sociological social psychology include Herbert Spencer, Karl Marx, Emile Durkheim, Max Weber, and Georg Simmel. Herbert Spencer's contribution to sociological social psychology included an examination of the creation and elaboration of social structures. In particular, he argued that the processes of heterogeneity, integration, adaptation, and differentiation emerge during the growth of social systems.

The heritage of sociological social psychology also includes Karl Marx's belief that the labor process is a social phenomenon and that people are importantly influenced by the economic mode of production. Marx emphasized the primacy of social class and he recognized that conflict is an important dynamic influence in society. Also, he refuted the widely accepted idea that social change was an evolutionary process.

Emile Durkheim's contributions to sociology, and ultimately sociological social psychology, include his emphasis on social facts as explanations for individual behavior and his argument that each facet of society endures because it serves some function. He also contributed unique insights regarding the importance of social integration. He believed that individuals become human in the process of social interaction. Individuals who are not integrated into the social system through social interaction experience anomie--a condition in which standards of conduct are weak or absent.

Max Weber's legacy includes the recognition that people's views of the world are subjective and their interpretations of reality furnish keys to their actions. He insisted that acts be explained by placing them in their social context. Weber also made major contributions to our understanding of prestige and power and their relevance to the definition of socioeconomic status. His pioneering work on stratification delineated the processes that influence stability and discrimination within stratification systems.

Georg Simmel's contributions include his emphasis on the effects of social interaction on the individual and his belief that groups are a necessary condition for the creation of society. He devoted particular attention to the relationship between group affiliations and social differentiation. Simmel was among the first to explore the principles of social exchange and to discuss the probable integrative and divisive consequences of intergroup conflict.

This sociological intellectual heritage can be discerned in a myriad of ways in modern sociological social psychology. To give only a few of many possible examples, Spencer's legacy can be seen among adherents of the social structure and personality school in their emphasis on reciprocal causation between the individual and the society and also in studies of leadership and social control.

Marx's influence can be seen in the focus on social class as an important mechanism by which social structure influences individual behavior and in recent nonevolutionary models of social change. His influence also appears in the conflict and labeling theory perspectives on the effects of power and status on individuals' life chances.

Durkheim's insights can be seen in the focus on social facts as explanations for individual behavior and in continued work on anomie and social control. The symbolic interactionist focus on the development of the self and society through social interaction also owes much to Durkheim.

Weber's legacy can be seen in the symbolic interactionist emphasis on the subjective construction of reality, the overall emphasis in the discipline on the reciprocity between the individual and the society, and in the continued focus in sociological social psychology on systems of stratification as important antecedents of individual and group behavior.

Simmel also contributed to the symbolic interactionist concern with social interaction and subjective meaning. Additionally, his influence has been felt in the study of social groups, social exchange, group affiliation, and social networks.

The early sociological emphasis on the interdependence of the individual and society remains in this sociological definition:

> Social psychology...is concerned with the behavior and psychological processes of individuals who occupy positions in social structures, organizations, and groups. On the one hand, social psychology is focused upon explaining the behavior of individuals as it is controlled, influenced, or limited by the social environment. On the other hand, it is concerned with the manner in which the behavior of individuals reacts upon, shapes, and alters social structures and enters into the functioning of groups (Lindesmith & Strauss, 1968).

Psychological Heritage. The nineteenth century intellectual roots of psychological social psychology include the work of Sir Francis Galton, Wilhelm Wundt, Ivan Pavlov, Sigmund Freud, and Max Wertheimer. Sir Francis Galton's contributions to psychological social psychology include the use and discovery of new statistical methods and his concern with intelligence and its consequences. His work on the heritability of human ability and individual differences has also had an enduring impact on the field.

One of Wilhelm Wundt's legacies was his dedication to the use of laboratory experimentation and quantitative procedures. He believed in the primacy of experience and therefore focused on consciousness, particularly the relationship of sensations to feelings, the measurement of mental processes through reaction time, and the processes of learning, memory, and recall.

Ivan Pavlov's impact on psychological social psychology is primarily due to his seminal behaviorist work on conditioned reflexes. He was the first to discover higher-order conditioning--a conditioned stimulus acquiring the capacity to serve as an unconditioned stimulus; stimulus generalization--generalization of a conditioned response to a different but similar stimulus; and discrimination--the process by which similar stimuli are distinguished.

Sigmund Freud's legacy to social psychology includes an emphasis on unconscious motives and how they control human behavior. He was among the first to recognize the basic conflict between society's needs and individual gratification. Among his other influential ideas were the concept of identification as a motivating force, the view of conscience as a cultural creation, and his discovery of the defense mechanisms people use to control anxiety.

Max Wertheimer's impact on psychological social psychology may be attributed to his concern with the *Gestalt*, or total situation, in understanding behavior. He believed the whole is greater than the sum of its parts, which led him to study principles of perceptual organization. In addition, he was concerned with the relationship between psychological and neurological processes.

The following examples illustrate a few of the many ways in which the intellectual heritage of psychological social psychology survives today. Galton's influence can be seen in the use of statistical techniques, the continued focus on intelligence, and the interest in partialling genetic from environmental explanations for behavior.

Wundt's heritage includes the tightly controlled experimental methods of psychological social psychology, its ongoing concern with the relationship between cognitions and emotions, and the use of concepts derived from learning in research conducted by psychological social psychologists.

Freud's influence continues to be felt in psychological social psychology's emphasis on motivation--particularly motivational factors that operate outside of an individual's awareness. There is also a continuing interest in identification and its consequences that can be traced to Freud.

Wertheimer's emphasis on the Gestalt can be seen in psychological social psychology's concern with the influence of the total situation on the individual. In a more indirect fashion, the current focus on the influence of cognition on perception owes much to Wertheimer.

Psychology's concern with the inner processes of individuals and the influence of the situation on individual's thoughts, feelings, and behaviors can be seen in a psychological definition of social psychology:

> [Social psychology is] an attempt to understand and explain how the thoughts, feelings, and behaviors of individuals are influenced by the actual, imagined, or implied presence of others (Allport, 1968/1985).

This discussion of differences in intellectual heritage and modern concerns also points up some of the similarities between sociological social psychology and psychological social psychology in definition, level of analysis, content and methodology. In fact, considerable overlap exists in all of these areas. We will consider definitions first. We believe that most social psychologists from sociology and psychology would accept the following definition of social psychology:

> Social psychology seeks to understand and explain human behavior in its social context. Social psychology is concerned with how people, and the social forces that impinge on them, affect one another (Rosenberg & Turner, 1981).

This definition encompasses sociology's concern with the reciprocal influence of the individual and the society. It also includes psychology's focus on the situation and its emphasis on cognitions and affect, as well as behavior. This definition is broad enough to include symbolic interactionism's studies of social interaction, the personality and social structure school's linkage of the macro- and micro-level of analysis, and psychological social psychology's work on social influence and social cognition.

When we examine level of analysis we see that while the discipline of sociology is a macro-level social science and psychology is a micro-level social science, this dichotomy breaks down in the case of the two social psychologies. Social psychology is generally considered to be conducted at the micro level of analysis, even within sociology, although sociologists from the social structure and personality tradition and the more structural symbolic interactionists study the relationship between micro-social and macro-social events.

Turning to the methodological differences between the two approaches, the common characterization of sociological social psychology as being qualitative and psychological social psychology as being quantitative denies the extensive use of sophisticated statistical techniques in sociological social psychology. Similarly, it ignores the occasional but increasing use of qualitative and archival techniques in psychological social psychology, for instance, the study of mental institutions by Rosenhan (1973) (see also Schofield, 1982; Simonton, 1981; Tetlock & McGuire, 1985). It further ignores the division within sociological social psychology into symbolic interactionism and the social structure and personality perspective, which relies heavily on quantitative methods. As House (1977) persuasively argues, there are not two but three social psychologies, and the differences between the two schools of sociological social psychology are substantial, although lessening. The qualitative/quantitative division also denies the existence of the tradition begun by the Iowa school of symbolic interactionism and continued today by structural symbolic interactionists, who make considerable use of quantitative methods.

We contend that the acquisition and dissemination of knowledge from only one of the social psychologies is parochial and harmful to the overriding goal of both social psychologies: understanding human behavior in its social context. The two approaches provide complementary information about the same problems. For instance, sociologists' demographic and survey studies of crowding (e.g., Gove, Hughes, & Galle, 1979) nicely converge with psychologists' laboratory studies conducted on the same issue (e.g, Schmidt & Keating, 1979). Similarly, sociological surveys of racial attitudes (e.g., Bobo, 1988; Farley, 1985) fit in interesting ways with psychological studies of modern or symbolic racism (e.g., McConahay, 1986; Dovidio & Gaertner, 1986).

Each of the social psychologies has methodological and theoretical strengths and weaknesses; a combination of approaches counterbalances some of the weaknesses of each school with the strengths of the other. For example, the symbolic interactionist focus on social interaction complements the micro-level focus in psychological social psychology because the latter typically does not take the point of view of the interacting individual into account. The combined information derived from the symbolic interactionists' study of explanations for behavior with its emphasis on the analysis of accounts and the psychological social psychologists' study of causal attributions illustrates this point (Kelley, 1967; Scott & Lyman, 1968; Weiner, 1986). Similarly, the micro-level analyses of the symbolic interactionists and psychological social psychologists are broadened by the linking of micro-level phenomena to macro-level phenomena by those from the social structure and personality school. Studies of the relationship between social class, socialization practices, and occupational self direction provide an example of the unique ways in which the social structure and personality school allows individual and group behavior to be placed in its broader structural context (Kohn & Schooler, 1978; Miller, Schooler, Kohn, & Miller, 1979).

To summarize briefly, we see the following advantage of the complementary methodologies of sociological and psychological social psychology. The ability to generalize from a sample to a population in survey research is supplemented by the control possible in experimentation. The richness of the qualitative data gained from observation and unstructured interviews provides a unique perspective missing from the quantitative data gained from experimentation. Differing methodologies provide a number of perspectives on a topic, and these multiple perspectives are an inherent characteristic of knowledge (Georgoudi & Rosnow, 1985). In the same way, our overlapping but somewhat different views of the content of social psychology broaden our knowledge and allow us to view a single topic from a variety of perspectives.

We further believe that the two social psychologies have never been more similar. Increasingly, as sociology has become more quantitatively sophisticated and as psychology has become more concerned with cognition, the subject matter, methods, and theories of the two social psychologies overlap. While the two social psychologies have always shared a perception of the social world as being subjective (Cartwright, 1979), until recently psychologists did not emphasize this point.

In addition, we believe that the practitioners of the two social psychologies have never been more interested in interchange between the disciplines. Widespread dissatisfaction with fragmentation of knowledge was a major contributing factor to the feeling of crisis in the social psychologies in the 1970s (Ring, 1967; Hendrick, 1977). This self-analytical period made members of both disciplines more open to different approaches. An increasing concern in both disciplines regarding the lack of range and scope of theory in social psychology

(Ring, 1967; Katz, 1972), the historical, national, and cultural limitations of our conclusions (Gergen, 1973; Hogan & Emler, 1978; Kohn, 1987), the lack of social significance of our endeavors (House, 1977; Smith, 1972) and the limitations of positivism (Harre & Secord, 1972; Secord, 1986; Pettigrew, this volume), likewise, have provided a renewed interest in alternative perspectives. Many social psychologists from both disciplines now define the content of social psychology more broadly than in the past and, concomitantly, use a greater range of the available methodological and statistical tools.

The Content of This Book

We turn now to the other chapters in the book, to see what these scholars from the social psychologies believe the two disciplines have to offer each other, what they consider to be the barriers to fruitful interchange and how they believe these barriers can be overcome.

In chapter 2, "Toward Unity and Bold Theory: Popperian Suggestions for Two Persistent Problems of Social Psychology," Thomas F. Pettigrew places the division of the social psychologies in the context of contemporary philosophy of science. He discusses two problems confronting the emergence of a single social psychology: lack of unity of its three contrasting branches (psychological social psychology, social structure and personality, symbolic interactionism) and the paucity of social psychological theory. Using Popper's philosophy of science, Pettigrew makes several suggestions for the solutions to these problems. These suggestions include the acceptance of a broad Popperian perspective in all the social psychologies that would help unify them and the development of more comprehensive interdisciplinary theories (bold theories in Popperian terms) linking the micro- and macro-levels of analysis.

In chapter 3, "Social Psychology at the Crossroads," Cookie White Stephan and Walter G. Stephan focus on the barriers to interchange between the disciplines of psychology and sociology. These barriers include stereotypes, the use of shared terms that do not have shared meanings, misconceptions regarding the subject matter of the other discipline, and differences in goals. They offer an intergroup relations explanation for the negative relationships that have sometimes existed between these two distinct groups. Stephan and Stephan also draw on the intergroup relations literature to suggest remedies for these negative relations, including increased intergroup contact, increased knowledge across groups through joint research projects, interdisciplinary training of students, and a multidisciplinary newsletter.

In chapter 4, "Sociology, Psychology, and Social Psychology (and Social Science)," James S. House addresses the following issues: What is social psychology? Why should we unify social psychology? How should we unify social psychology? Are we making progress in unifying social psychology? House argues that a unified social psychology must include biology as well as sociology and psychology. He believes that unity among the various branches of social psychology is needed because the growing specialization in social psychology impedes its overall purpose of understanding social phenomena. House feels this unification can best be accomplished by a focus on real world problems, and through interdisciplinary and problem-focused training and professional structures.

In chapter 5, "Interdisciplinary Social Psychology: Prospects and Problems," Carl W. Backman notes several trends underlying a growing convergence between the sociological and psychological traditions in social psychology. One such trend involves the emergence of a new paradigm within the psychological tradition that is very similar to that long held by sociologists. A second development consists of an increasing interest on the part of those in psychology in a number of research interests that historically have been of more concern to sociologists. Backman argues that these trends should be expanded and suggests that the process and structure of communication in social psychology be altered. Backman's suggestions include cross-disciplinary training, professional journals, and professional meetings.

In chapter 6, Carmi Schooler's "Interdisciplinary Lessons: The Two Social Psychologies from the Perspective of a Psychologist Practicing Sociology," maintains that the two social psychologies have much to learn from one another, with strengths of each field available to compensate for weaknesses in the other. He argues for a greater concern with describing mechanisms at the proper level of specificity and understanding the differences in organizing principles that exist among different levels of phenomena. Schooler believes attention to these concerns will not only help social psychologists understand the level at which research should be carried out given the questions asked, but will also show them the relevance of the other discipline's work at different levels of specificity that employ different organizing principles.

Chapter 7, "Consequences of the Gap between the 'Two Social Psychologies'" consists of Sheldon Stryker's argument that structural barriers between the disciplines of psychology and sociology have had positive as well as negative consequences for social psychology. He believes a true merger to be impossible due to institutional separation. Were it possible, Stryker posits the disappearance of sociological social psychology. This disappearance would be a result of the size of psychological relative to sociological social psychology. In addition, he argues that a creative tension between the disciplines benefits the social psychology of both and avoids the potential for their bland homogenization.

Finally, in chapter 8, "Is Unity Possible? A Summary," Thomas F. Pettigrew draws together the common strands of the preceding chapters. He summarizes the barriers to and gains of a more unified social psychology, and urges social psychologists from both disciplines to continue to work toward synthesis. Finally, Pettigrew assesses our progress toward unifying the social psychologies, and offers proposals for further unification.

References

Allport, G. W. (1985). The historical background of social psychology. In G. Lindzey & E. Aronson (Eds.), *Handbook of social psychology* (Vol. 1). New York: Random House.

Bobo, L. (1988). Symbolic racism. In P. A. Katz & D. A. Taylor (Eds.), *Eliminating racism: Profiles in controversy*. New York: Plenum.

Cartwright, D. (1979). Contemporary social psychology in historical perspective. *Social Psychology Quarterly*, *42*, 82-93.

Dovidio, J., & Gaertner, S. L. (Eds.). (1956). *Prejudice, discrimination, and racism*. Orlando: Academic Press.

Farley, R. (1985). Three steps forward and two back? Recent changes in the social and economic status of blacks. In R. D. Alba (Ed.), *Ethnicity and race in the U.S.A.* Boston: Routledge & Kegan Paul.

Gergen, K. J. (1973). Social psychology as history. *Journal of Personality and Social Psychology*, *26*, 309-320.

Georgoudi, M., & Rosnow, R. L. (1985). Notes toward a contextualist understanding of social psychology. *Personality and Social Psychology Bulletin*, *11*, 5-22.

Gove, W. R., Hughes, M., & Galle, O. R. (1979). Overcrowding in the home: An empirical investigation of it possible pathological consequences. *American Sociological Review*, *44*, 59-80.

Harre, R., & Secord, P. F. (1972). *The explanation of social behavior*. Totowa, NJ: Rowman & Littlefield.

Hendrick, C. (1977). Social psychology as an experimental science. In C. Hendrick (Ed.), *Perspective on social psychology*. Hillsdale, NJ: Erlbaum.

Hogan, R. T., & Emler, N. P. (1978). The biases in contemporary social psychology. *Social Research*, *45*, 478-534.

House, J. S. (1977). The three faces of social psychology. *Sociometry*, *40*, 161-177.

Katz, D. (1972). Some final considerations about experimentation in social psychology. In C. G. McClintock (Ed.), *Experimental social psychology*. New York: Holt, Rinehart, & Winston.

Kelley, H. H. (1967). Attribution theory in social psychology. In H. Levine (Ed.), *Nebraska symposium on motivation*. Lincoln, NB: University of Nebraska Press.

Kohn, M. L. (1987). Cross-national research as an analytic strategy. *American Sociological Review*, *52*, 713-731.

Kohn, M. L., & Schooler, C. (1978). The reciprocal effects of the substantive complexity of work and intellectual flexibility: A longitudinal assessment. *American Journal of Sociology*, *84*, 24-52.

Lindesmith, A. R., & Strauss, A. L. (1968). *Social psychology* (3rd ed.). New York: Holt, Rinehart, & Winston.

McConahay, J. B. (1986). Modern racism, ambivalence, and the Modern Racism Scale. In J. F. Dovidio & S. L. Gaertner (Eds.), *Prejudice, discrimination, and racism*. New York: Academic Press.

McDougall, W. (1908). *An introduction to social psychology*. London: Methuen.

Miller, J., Schooler, C., Kohn, M. L., & Miller, K. A. (1979). Women and work: The psychological effects of occupational conditions. *American Journal of Sociology, 5*, 66-91.

Ring, K. (1967). Experimental social psychology: Some sober questions about frivolous values. *Journal of Experimental Social Psychology, 3*, 113-123.

Rosenberg, M., and Turner, R. H. (1981). *Social psychology: Sociological perspectives.* New York: Basic Books.

Rosenhan, D. L. (1973). On being sane in insane places. *Science, 173*, 250-258.

Ross, E. A. (1908). *Social psychology: An outline and source book.* New York: Macmillan.

Scott, M. D. & Lyman, S. M. (1968). Accounts. *American Sociological Review, 33*, 46-62.

Secord, P. F. (1986). Social psychology as a science. In J. Margolis, P. T. Manicas, R. Harre, & P. F. Secord (Eds.), *Psychology: Designing the discipline.* Oxford: Basil Blackwell.

Schmidt, D. E. & Keating, J. P. (1979). Human crowding and personal control: an integration of research. *Psychological Bulletin, 86*, 680-700.

Schofield. J. W. (1982). *Black and white in school: Trust, tension or tolerance.* New York: Praeger.

Simonton, D. K. (1981). The library laboratory: archival data in personality and social psychology. In L. Wheeler (Ed.), *Review of personality and social psychology, 2*, 217-243. Beverly Hills, CA: Sage.

Smith, M. B. (1972). Is experimental social psychology advancing? Journal of *Experimental Social Psychology, 8*, 86-96.

Tetlock, P. E., & McGuire, C. B. (1985). Integrative complexity of Soviet rhetoric as a predictor of Soviet foreign policy behavior. *International Journal of Group Tensions, 14*, 113-128.

Triplett, N. (1897). The dynamogenic factors in pacemaking and competition. *American Journal of Psychology, 9*, 507-533.

Weiner, B. (1986). *An attributionaltheoryofemotion and motivation.* New York: Springer-Verlag.

2
Toward Unity and Bold Theory: Popperian Suggestions for Two Persistent Problems of Social Psychology

Thomas F. Pettigrew

Introduction

Two persistent and interrelated problems confront the emergence of a broad-based, multimethod discipline of social psychology. The first is unity between its contrasting branches--symbolic interactionism, contextual social psychology, and experimental social psychology. The second problem is the general paucity throughout social psychology of bold theory that can be tested and falsified. This chapter briefly considers each of these problems, and ventures several suggestions toward their solution from the perspective of Karl Popper's integrated philosophies of knowledge and science (Ackermann, 1976; Burke, 1983; Currie & Musgrave, 1985; Levinson, 1982; Magee, 1973; Miller, 1985; O'Hear, 1980; Popper, 1950, 1959, 1968, 1976). [1]

Unity of the Discipline

Several writers (Backman, 1983; House, 1977; Pettigrew, 1980) note that social psychology is severely split into three camps. Two branches are highly mobilized and distinctly different. Symbolic interactionism rejects positivism emphatically. Found almost exclusively in sociology departments, it often maximizes external validity at the expense of internal validity by surrendering research rigor to get close to the action and concerns of the "real world." By contrast, experimental social psychology adopted much of the Vienna-circle positivism of its chief model, experimental psychology. Rarely found outside of psychology departments, this branch maximizes internal validity at the expense of external validity by restricting itself largely to student subjects in college laboratory settings. Neither of these branches tend to follow the work of the other, though increasingly their interests and even their research findings have been converging. Indeed, the principal contentions of symbolic interactionism concerning the subtle, reflexive processes of human interaction have during the past decade received research support from the very experimental methods that the branch rejected (e.g., Snyder et al., 1977; Word et al., 1974).

The third subgroup of the discipline is the least mobilized and recognized. Its proponents are found in both sociology and psychology departments as well as in interdisciplinary and applied settings. As the central branch with representation in both originating disciplines, it has more communication with the other branches of the discipline. And its adherents are the ones who most often advocate unity of the field; indeed, all but Walter Stephan and Sheldon Stryker of this volume's authors fall largely within this branch. Various labels have been applied to this group over the years; "social structure and personality" and "psychological sociology" are used in other chapters of this volume. But we shall refer to it as *contextual* social psychology, since it is distinctive in its attention to individual factors in the context of macro-structural factors. Operationally, it is best defined, perhaps, as the branch that comprises most of the membership of the Social Psychology Section of the American Sociological Association and the basic constituency for the *Social Psychological Quarterly*.

Contextual social psychology shares with experimental social psychology a concern with quantitative methods and with symbolic interactionism a concern for real-world data and applied problems. More than the other branches, however, it is interested in both general personality and social structural considerations and more actively seeks to specify the mediators between these levels. This combination of concerns usually dictates a trade-off between external and internal validity--thus, this branch makes greater use of quasi-experimental and nonexperimental methods, especially surveys using probability samples.

In spite of departmental and other structural barriers between them described in detail throughout this volume, major convergencies have emerged in recent years across the branches. Thus, all three (1) reject unitary trait conceptions and emphasize (2) cognitive approaches, (3) the reactivity of social interaction, and (4) the power of situations to shape behavior. In addition, (5) numerous middle-range theories have diffused across the branches--from labeling and exchange theories to conceptions of distributive justice and social evaluation. Significantly, for the first time in three editions, the experimentally-oriented

Handbook of Social Psychology (Lindzey & Aronson, 1985) included a chapter on symbolic interactionism (Stryker & Statham, 1985) and another on deviance (Archer, 1985). Later chapters in this volume cite many other convergencies. And it is these convergencies and the development of increasingly distinctive theory and methods upon which rests social psychology's claim to be an emerging discipline.

But we should not exaggerate these convergencies. The two most divergent branches, symbolic interactionism and experimental social psychology, still routinely reject each other. For example, Hewitt (1976, 1979), in the first three pages of the two editions of his symbolic interactionist textbook, dismisses as irrelevant *all* social psychology found in psychology departments. Likewise, Jones (1985), in his *Handbook* chapter on "major developments in social psychology during the past five decades," views the field as part of psychology and thereby explicitly excludes all social psychological work done in sociology. "The overlap in empirical content" in the social psychological work done in the two root disciplines, he writes, "may reflect superficial similarities that gloss over distinct analytic differences" (Jones, 1985:50). He provides no examples of his position nor does he cite the sociological equivalent to the *Handbook*, Rosenberg and Turner's (1981) *Social Psychology: Sociological Perspectives*. He also omits *Symbolic Interaction* and *Social Problems* from his listing of social psychological journals. Yet Jones, a careful scholar, does make use of sociological sources. Thus, he holds the famous W. I. Thomas subjectivist dictum (Thomas & Thomas, 1928:572) to be basic to social psychological thought, notes the comparable exchange theory ideas of Homans and of Thibaut and Kelley (1959), and cites several empirical sociological studies.

Why this mutual rejection? The following chapters specify an array of factors that help to explain this mirrored disregard. Here we shall focus upon a fundamental reason that underlies much of the mutual rejection--the radically diverse epistomologies that separate the branches. It is this conflict in perspectives that underlies the "distinct analytic differences" which Jones regards as so obvious as not to require explanation or evidence. In turn, many symbolic interactionists regard positivism as simply incapable of uncovering the subtleties of human interaction. And many experimental social psychologists identify "science" with an implicit Vienna-circle positivism that pervades their thought and theory. From these contrasting perspectives, there is little wonder that they seldom read one another.

Two questions arise at this point. The first is to ask why this disunity between the various branches of social psychology should be perceived as a "problem." Why even produce a volume such as this one around the topic? If the branches differ in such a fundamental respect, why not agree with Hewitt and Jones, accept these branches as forever separate and incomparable enterprises, and give up the aim of ever "uniting" the various social scientists who happen to label themselves "social psychologists?"

This is a fair question; and it is addressed repeatedly throughout this book. For myself, I believe that the various branches have set similar goals for themselves, that the many convergences between them in recent years are not in the least "superficial," and that each of the three branches would be significantly strengthened by the theory and methods of the other two. Indeed, their convergences are made all the more remarkable and impressive by the sharp differences between them. In a real sense, each of the distinctive branches complements the others; with greater coordination between them, they could together form a discipline of considerable range and depth in both method and theory.

This raises the second question. What epistemological compromise would provide an open and broad enough umbrella for three such dissimilar branches? Perhaps, there is none. But I wish audaciously to propose one: the critical rationalism of Sir Karl Popper. Without attempting a full summary of this philosophical system, let me review several highlights of Popper's position that commend its use for this purpose.

"At a time when most philosophers of science are inductivist, subjectivist, positivist, instrumentalist, behaviorist, materialist, monistic," writes Bartley (1982:267), "Popper is deductivist, realist, anti-positivist, anti-instrumentalist, anti-behaviorist, anti-materialist, interactionist." Popper's position is grounded on seven consistent assertions. (1) He denies the existence of induction. Impressed by the achievements of Kepler, Galileo, Newton, Maxwell, and Einstein, he believes science follows a basically deductive cycle: problem, tentative solution or theory, test, new problems uncovered, etc. (2) The critical feature of this cycle is its trial and error character. Impressed by Darwinian evolution in biology, Popper holds that ideas follow a similar development. (3) The decisive demarcation of science from nonscience is not inductive verification, as traditional positivists maintain, but deductive falsification. An infinite number of verifications do not prove a principle, but one false instance disproves it. Scientific truth exists, he asserts, but we can never be certain when we have uncovered it. Consequently, the best we can do is to approach it through the repeated elimination of plausible rival hypotheses.

(4) Metaphysics, which is not falsifiable, is none the less an invaluable source for scientific ideas and theories. This openness to nonscience is one of the attractive features of Popper's thinking. It denies Snow's two-worlds thesis of science *versus* humanism; and it liberates the imagination from the narrow Baconian model of conventional positivism. (5) We should not be "over-fussy" about language (Miller, 1985:192). Singularly *un*impressed by the contentions of the later Wittgenstein, Popper assumes a refreshing posture: "Never let yourself be goaded into taking seriously problems about words and their meanings. What must be taken seriously are questions of fact, and assertions about facts: theories and hypotheses; the problems they solve; and the problems they raise." (Popper, 1976:19).

(6) It is useful to think of three, highly interactive "worlds." World 1 is the physical world; World 2 is the subjective world of human thought and experience; and World 3 consists of the products of human thought. Like social psychologists, Popper is fascinated by the fact that World 3, once established, becomes an objective part of social reality that shapes social life and history.

Finally, (7) Popper believes passionately in the efficacy of open, critical debate. Impressed by what he conjectures to be the secret behind the intellectual progress of the presocratic, Milesian Greek philosophers, he regards the systematic use of critical discussion to be essential to scientific advance. This leads him to advocate that scientists stick their necks out, invite criticism, and expect to be shown to be wrong. Bold theories, that convey more content but risk falsification, are much to be preferred to trivial, timid ideas--a point to which we shall return.

While the rigid formats of the *Journal of Personality and Social Psychology* and the *Journal of Experimental Social Psychology* provide no hint of it, experimental social psychology has been moving increasingly toward a broader, more Popperian perspective. Contextual social psychology, with its greater emphasis on applied and field research, has long been more explicitly Popperian. Thus, it is not surprising that the leading Popperian in American social science, Donald Campbell, is an honored figure in both experimental and contextual social psychology. Many of Campbell's most noted innovations--such as quasi-experimental methods and his call for "an experimenting society"--are highly Popperian in character and widely embraced in the discipline.

Several recent innovations reflect this growing, if often unwitting, acceptance of a Popperian stance. Breaking out of the straight-laced journal formats that characterize the discipline, George Levinger

(1987), the then-editor of the *Journal of Social Issues*, introduced a "dialogue" format for his publication. He published only two papers on a central topic--in the first instance, the focus was on black American employment problems. But the same issue also contained nine searching critiques of the papers by a wide variety of specialists followed by rejoinders from the original authors. It constituted, then, a straight-forward operationalization of Popper's insistence that probing critiques and debates among specialists is a necessary condition for scientific progress. The format recalled the Lewinian tradition of *quasselstrippe*--the institutionalized critical discussion among faculty and students on a regular basis with evening meetings. Indeed, Lewin, like Popper, came of intellectual age in Central Europe between the world wars; and many aspects of his training, methods and theory bear close relationship to Popperian contentions.

The enormous and sudden popularity of meta-analyses reveals a more widespread, Popperian-like trend in both experimental and contextual social psychology. Though its most modern form and label were introduced by an educational psychologist (Glass, 1976, 1977), both experimental and contextual social psychologists are disproportionately utilizing the method. A glance at almost any issue of the *Psychological Bulletin* reveals this trend, not to mention the many meta-analyses now published directly in social psychological journals. Some of this rapid popularity probably reflects the field's yearning for closure, for clues to broader theory--to which we shall turn shortly. But there is also an implicit acceptance of Popper's evolutionary view of science involved in this widespread use of meta-analyses. Vienna-circle positivism typically calls for incremental changes in repeated studies on a phenomenon so as to isolate, one by one, the key independent variables. But meta-analysis thrives in evaluating research literatures that boast somewhat diverse methods and measures--a situation that reflects more closely the evolutionary notions of Karl Popper. To be sure, meta-analysis is often criticized by traditional positivists for "mixing oranges and apples" (Mullen, 1989: Chapter 10). But Popperians can counter by pointing to the celebrated instances of where the incremental change strategy slowed progress because of similarities in research design across an entire literature. The famous instance of the risky shift group phenomenon comes to mind (Cartwright, 1973; Jones, 1985:58).

But there is little evidence of Popperian influence yet in symbolic interactionism. I believe a more explicit use of Popper's system in the experimental and contextual branches of social psychology would make a rapprochement with symbolic interactionism far easier, if for no other reason that it would signal a more open, flexible notion of what science is and is about. But I concede that acceptance of many of Popper's strictures by symbolic interactionists might be difficult, though a distinction must be made between the branch's method and theory in contrast to its dominant political stance. Put bluntly, I believe that there is no fundamental conflict between Popper's views and the actual scientific practice of symbolic interactionism; but, to the extent that symbolic interactionists regard themselves in the critical school of sociology, there is a genuine clash between political perspectives.

As documented in several chapters of this book, the variety of methods used by current symbolic interactionists has greatly expanded in recent years. Yet the most traditional form of field work in symbolic interactionism is often regarded as an inductive enterprise. But I believe that it is more precisely described in Popper's terms: a constant trial-and-error process between problems and tentative explanations on the one hand and the observations on the other. The struggles between investigators and their field notes, so well described by workers in this tradition, are in my view valuable micro-descriptions of the many complex interactions between Popper's Worlds 2 and 3. I do not regard Popper's limited version of anti-subjectivism as an impediment to the particular type of subjectivism advanced by all branches of social psychology. On the contrary, I suspect Popper's realism could sharpen social psychological thought on precisely what the Thomas dictum means and implies.

It is conflicting political perspectives that raise the more difficult problem. A 1961 conference on the logic of the social sciences at Tubingen was the occasion of a confrontation between Popper and T. W. Adorno of the Frankfort School, a confrontation that sharply exposes the conflict between the liberal democratic and critical political perspectives. For members of the critical school, such as Adorno, Popper's views are simply a variation of modern positivism, for they define a positivist as "anyone who accepts the appearance of society as social reality." (Ackermann, 1985:177). Popper's support of "piecemeal social engineering" and his beliefs in open discussion, compromise, and the democratic process make him seem hopelessly naive in the eyes of many critical theorists. Though not myself in the critical camp, I too regard some of Popper's social commentary as well-meaning but mistaken--probably reflecting his political disillusionments in the turbulent Vienna of the 1920s and 1930s, first with the Communists and then with the Social Democrats (Popper, 1976). But I do not find acceptance of his politics to be a necessary condition for acceptance of his basic contributions to epistemology.

We turn now to a second persistent problem of all of social psychology's branches--the lack of broad yet falsifiable theory.

The Need for Bold, Falsifiable Theory

Social psychological theory fails to live up to the field's ambitions. Whether we regard this situation as a "crisis," a scientific shortcoming, or just an embarrassment, social psychologists are in general agreement that our models and even our approaches to theory are in need of major reassessment.

Most social psychological "theories" are actually frameworks or general perspectives, not theories in the full sense of being testable propositions capable of being empirically falsified (Popper, 1959). And these frameworks in recent decades have emphasized cognitive and slighted emotional factors. They typically stress similarity (mechanical solidarity) and ignore the socially binding significance of differences (organic solidarity)--Durkheim's other side of social life. They are largely static rather than dynamic. As such, they tend to emphasize isolated, rather than cumulative, effects--a reflection of the widespread use of cross-sectional research designs. Social psychological theories also tend to assume universality even though their tests rarely sample times, situations, and cultures. Indeed, they are routinely conceptualized and demonstrated in Western and especially North American cultural terms. [2]

To sum up, five interrelated weaknesses of current social psychological theory can be advanced. With notable exceptions, social psychological theories:

1. Are more often loose frameworks than testable theories;
2. Have centered on cold cognition to the relative exclusion of affective considerations;
3. Stress similarities (mechanical solidarity) to the virtual exclusion of differences (organic solidarity) as social bonds;
4. Focus largely on isolated, non-cumulative effects;
5. Too glibly assume universality across time, situations, and cultures.

Each of these particular criticisms is in turn a special case of a more fundamental weakness: the absence of generic theory in social psychology that links the various levels of analysis. The field provides to date only narrow-to-middle-range theories. It has yet to follow Popper's principle of preference: choose "a theory with the greater informative content, ...even before it has been tested, [to] a theory with little content" (Miller, 1985:112). This bold strategy of theory construction not only holds out greater hope for major advances, but it addresses the widely recognized problem of the near-impossibility of falsifying much of social psychological theory. Bold theories, as Popper emphasizes, permit more challenging tests, for they are more likely to be falsified. And even if falsified, Popper believes that we may well uncover more new and unexpected facts and "problems" in the falsification of bold theories than in the testing of theories with little content (Miller, 1985:112). In stark contrast to the principle of preference, social psychological ideas seem to be pursued in ever narrowing spirals that increasingly specify the mediating or moderating processes of one particular and limited phenomenon. The experimental social psychologist, Harold Kelley, speaks for many in all three branches of the field when he writes:

> The topics in social psychology read more like a Sears and Roebuck catalogue than like a novel. They provide a listing of items of possible interest to the reader rather than a story with a plot, development of characters, and so on. Our work is more like that of mining engineers, who find a vein of valuable material and dig it out, and not like the work of geologists, who identify various features of the earth, describe their interrelations, and explain their origins. These are ways of saying that we do not know the total list of the phenomena we are studying (what will be the popular motive next year?) and we do not know the interrelations among the various ones we have studied so far (what is their priority of hierarchical order, their underlying genotypic structure?) (Kelley, 1983:8-9).

While there is wide consensus on the existence of the problem, there is far less agreement as to its diagnosis and remedy. Given the interstitial nature of social psychology between the micro-level of the individual and the various macro-levels of collectivities, it is apparent that the search for Kelley's "underlying genotypic structure" must focus greater attention upon the situation. Experimental social psychology has for three decades been demonstrating in the laboratory the critical significance of the situation. This emphasis marks yet another growing convergence between the various branches of social psychology, for symbolic interactionists and other sociologically oriented social psychologists have long focused on the situation as a critical determinant of social behavior. Yet it took the dramatic findings of vivid experiments--from Asch on conformity followed by Milgram on obedience and Zimbardo on prisons--to establish situational factors as a potentially unifying focus for the field. Nonetheless, progress has been slow over the past generation. Social psychology has yet to produce an effective taxonomy of situations, or even establish their chief dimensions. Further, the field has not made many significant advances in isolating the mediating processes between individuals and situations.

Two directions are possible, indeed, both together are needed:

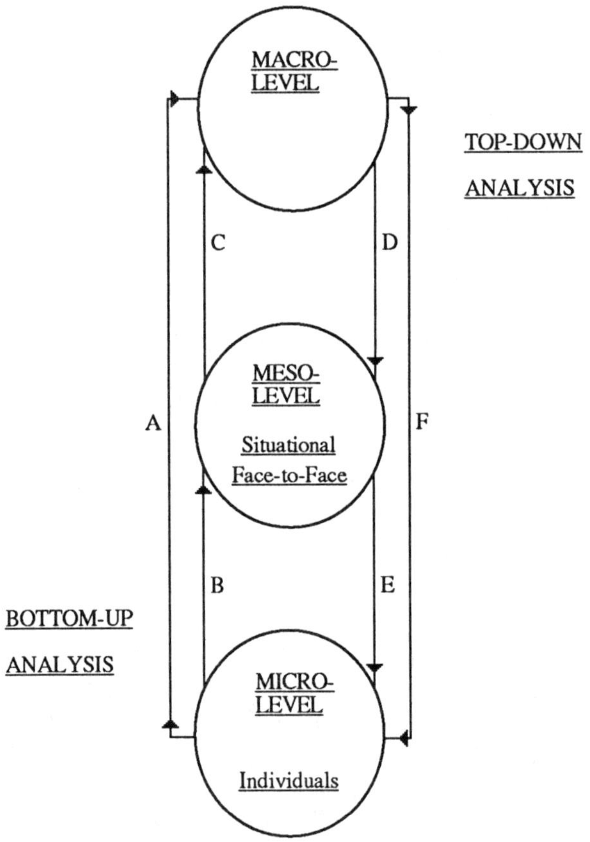

FIGURE 1. Six Types of Social Psychological Analysis

bottom-up analyses that begin at the micro level and link with salient features of situations and higher structures; and top-down analyses that begin at the macro levels, situational, institutional or societal, and link with individual characteristics. [3] Figure 1 indicates both of these analytic directions; and by linking the micro, meso (situational), and macro levels it reveals six basic causal paths. Paths A, B, and C are bottom-up, while D, E, and F are top-down analyses. The A path, unmediated effects from the individual to the macro level, is rarely found in social psychology. Perhaps, "great man" theories from history made them suspect. But institutional selection issues--how institutions are influenced by differential recruitment of individuals--deserve more attention from the discipline. The other unmediated path, F--from the macro to the micro-individual level, has received a bit more attention. Perhaps, the best known work here is Inkeles' ground-breaking research on individual modernity in six developing countries (Inkeles, 1978; Inkeles & Smith, 1974).

The disciplinary focus on the situation and face-to-face interaction ensures that paths B, C, D, and E will receive the major attention. In all three branches, however, the bulk of social psychological work consists of the B and E paths--links between the individual and situational levels of analysis--a relatively limited sampling of the possibilities. And when called on for practical advice in solving problems, the field generally makes a top-down recommendation utilizing path E: change something about the situation (increase choice, cease labeling practices, allow more participation, etc.) and micro-level changes are predicted (increased morale, less sense of being stigmatized, greater involvement, etc.).

But bolder theory is needed throughout the discipline, theory that involves more than one of these paths yet remains testable. All too often, I fear social psychological work fits Popper's critique against timid theories with little content. To be sure, we have numerous and interesting frameworks that are broad--such as labeling "theory" and attribution "theory." Yet these are not "bold" in the Popperian sense, for they offer a perspective but not rich and falsifiable content. They can be--and have been--easily patched up to withstand varied criticisms over time. This is not to say that such frameworks are not valuable. But it is to assert that we need to go beyond these formulations and pursue Popper's contention that we will learn far more from having our bold theories falsified than we will from failing to falsify narrow conceptions. Toward that end, Schooler advances in his chapter intriguing ideas from comparative psychology for a reconceptualization of levels of analysis.

A Final Word

But where will bold theories in the Popperian sense come from? It is here that my two theses come together. I believe the convergence of the three branches of social psychology will enable each to become bolder in their theoretical efforts. For example, one principal reason, in my view, for the much-discussed "crisis" in experimental social psychology during the 1970s was derived directly from the failure to nest its phenomena and theory in a broader social context (Pettigrew, 1988). The other two branches could help supply this. In return, experimental social psychology could help the other parts of the discipline to make their propositions more testable under controlled conditions. Symbolic interactionists like "the action" up close; experimentalists prefer the controlled setting of the laboratory. Kurt Lewin argued for the value of field and lab tests aiding each other. Now that the most fundamental features of symbolic interactionism are gaining support in laboratory tests, there is reason to expect that something resembling Lewin's ideas could become a more permanent feature of the social psychological enterprise.

In short, I believe that disunity within social psychology has deterred the development of both bold theory and a richer variety of interrelated research methods. Consequently, I dare hope that the present trend of convergence between the three sub-fields will develop the unity that will enable bold theory to begin to emerge. And I believe the ideas of Karl Popper can help toward this end.

Notes

[1] Two especially useful introductions to Popper's thought are provided by Magee's (1973) pointed outline and Miller's (1985) carefully edited volume of 30 brief selections drawn from throughout Popper's writings. Popper's (1976) autobiography and the supportive essays found in Levinson (1982) are also instructive. For critical reviews of Popper's system, see Ackermann (1976), O'Hear (1980), and Currie and Musgrave (1985)--the last of which focuses on Popper's relevance for "the human sciences." I have my own criticisms (largely concerning Popper's absolutist position against induction and the lack of a criterion by which falsification can be accepted as final).

[2] I omit Gergen's (1973) historical criticism of social psychological theory: "theories of social behavior are primarily reflections of contemporary history" and therefore their "premises are often invalidated" over time. At a broad level, this argument can be viewed as a special case of "historicism" in its least defensible form as extreme historical relativism (Meyerhoff, 1959). Together with most modern historians, I reject this perspective. But at a narrower level, Gergen's argument can be seen as a special case call for social psychological theory and research to be nested systematically in their macro-social contexts. In this second interpretation, I accept Gergen's criticism. But it is more precisely stated generically for the needed social contexts vary not only across time but across cultures and situations in the same time.

[3] Bales (1970) offers a rare and explicit attempt to include both approaches. While fundamentally a bottom-up theory, he ingeniously employs a three-dimensional-space analysis that focuses specifically on self-analytic groups. Within this situational context, Bales carefully developed over decades of theory-directed investigation a bold system that simultaneously looks at personality (as 27 interacting types), role structure (as with his famous distinction between task-oriented and socio-emotional roles), and group structure (with a direct analysis of group interaction). Significantly, Bales (1940) began his career by writing a Masters thesis on "The Concept 'Situation' as a Methodological Tool." The richness and rarity of Bales' important contribution supports the argument proposed in these pages; indeed, this work helped to shape these views.

References

Ackermann, R. J. (1976). *The philosophy of Karl Popper*. Amherst, MA: University of Massachusetts Press.

Ackermann, R. J. (1985). Popper and German social philosophy. In G. Currie & A. Musgrave (Eds.), *Popper and the human sciences*. Dordrecht, The Netherlands: Martinus Nijhoff.

Archer, D. (1985). Social deviance. In G. Lindzey & E. Aronson (Eds.), *Handbook of social psychology* (3rd ed.) (Vol. 2). New York: Random House.

Backman, C. W. (1983). Toward an interdisciplinary social psychology. In L. Berkowitz (Ed.), *Advances in experimental social psychology* (Vol. 16). New York: Academic Press.

Bales, R. F. (1940). *The concept "situation" as a methodological tool.* Unpublished Masters thesis, University of Oregon, Eugene.

Bales, R. F. (1970). *Personality and interpersonal behavior*. New York: Holt, Rinehart and Winston.

Bartley, W. W., III. (1982). A Popperian harvest. In P. Levinson (Ed.), *In pursuit of truth*. Atlantic Highlands, NJ: Humanities Press.

Burke, T. E. (1983). *The philosophy of Popper*. Manchester, England: Manchester University Press.

Cartwright, D. (1973). Determinants of scientific progress: The case of research on the risky shift. *American Psychologist, 28,* 222-231.

Currie, G., Musgrave, A. (Eds.). (1985). *Popper and the human sciences*. Dordrecht, Netherlands: Martinus Nijhoff.

Gergen, K. J. (1973). Social psychology as history. *Journal of Personality and Social Psychology, 26,* 309-320.

Glass, G. (1976). Primary, secondary and meta-analysis of research. *Educational Research, 5,* 3-8.

Glass, G. (1977). Integrating findings: The meta-analysis of research. *Review of Research in Education, 5,* 351-379.

Hewitt, J. P. (1976). *Self and society: A symbolic interactionist social psychology*. Boston: Allyn and Bacon.

Hewitt, J. P. (1979). *Self and society: A symbolic interactionist social psychology* (2nd ed.). Boston: Allyn and Bacon.

House, J. S. (1977). The three faces of social psychology. *Sociometry, 40,* 161-177.

Inkeles, A. (1978). National differences in individual modernity. *Comparative Studies in Sociology, 1,* 47-72.

Inkeles, A., & Smith, D. (1974). *Becoming modern: Individual change in six developing countries*. Cambridge, MA: Harvard University Press.

Jones, E. E. (1985). Major developments in social psychology during the past five decades. In G. Lindzey & E. Aronson (Eds.), *Handbook of social psychology* (3rd ed.) (Vol. 1). New York: Random House.

Kelley, H. H. (1983). The situational origins of human tendencies: A further reason for the formal analysis of structures. *Personality and Social Psychology Bulletin, 9,* 8-30.

Levinger, G. (Ed.). (1987). Black employment opportunities: Macro and micro perspectives. *Journal of Social Issues*, *43*, 1-156.
Levinson, P. (Ed.). (1982). *In pursuit of truth*. Atlantic Highlands, NJ: Humanities Press.
Lindzey, G. & Aronson, E. (Eds.). (1985). *Handbook of social psychology*. (3rd ed) (Vols. 1-2). New York: Random House.
Magee, B. (1973). *Popper*. New York: Viking.
Meyerhoff, H. (Ed.). (1959). *The philosophy of history in our time*. Garden City, NY: Doubleday.
Miller, D. (Ed.). (1985). *Popper selections*. Princeton, NJ: Princeton University Press.
Mullen, B. (1989). *Advanced BASIC meta-analysis*. Hillsdale, NJ: Erlbaum.
O'Hear, A. (1980). *Karl Popper*. London: Routledge & Kegan Paul.
Pettigrew, T. F. (1980). Social psychology's potential contributions to an understanding of poverty. In V. T. Covello (Ed.), *Poverty and public policy: An evaluation of social science research*. Boston: Hall.
Pettigrew, T. F. (1988). Influencing policy with social psychology. *Journal of Social Issues*, *44 (2)*, 205-219.
Popper, K. R. (1950). *The open society and its enemies*. Princeton, NJ: Princeton University Press.
Popper, K. R. (1959). *The logic of scientific discovery*. London: Hutchinson. (Originally published in German in 1934.)
Popper, K. R. (1968). *Conjectures and refutations*. New York: Harper & Row.
Popper, K. R. (1976). *Unended quest*. La Salle, IL: Open Court.
Rosenberg. M., & Turner, R. H. (Eds.). (1981). *Social psychology: Sociological perspectives*. New York: Basic Books.
Snyder, M. L., Tanke, E. D., & Berscheid, E. (1977). Social perception and interpersonal behavior: On the self-fulfilling nature of social stereotypes. *Journal of Personality and Social Psychology*, *35*, 656-666.
Stryker, S., & Statham, A. (1985). Symbolic interaction and role theory. In G. Lindzey & E. Aronson (Eds.), *Handbook of social psychology* (3rd ed) (Vol. 1). New York: Random House.
Thibaut, J. W., & Kelley, H. H. (1959). *The social psychology of groups*. New York: Wiley.
Thomas, W. I., & Thomas, D. S. (1928). *The child in America: Behavior problems and programs*. New York: Knopf.
Word, C. O., Zanna, M. P., & Cooper, J. (1974). The nonverbal mediation of self-fulfilling prophecies in interracial interaction. *Journal of Experimental Social Psychology*, *10*, 109-120.

3
Social Psychology at the Crossroads

Cookie White Stephan and Walter G. Stephan

More than 35 years ago Muzafer Sherif held a conference entitled "Social Psychology at the Crossroads" (Rohrer & Sherif, 1951). The crossroad to which he referred was the intersection between sociological social psychology (SSP) and psychological social psychology (PSP). The metaphor of an overpass might have been more appropriate, since the two disciplines seldom actually met. Recognizing that the two social psychologies had not achieved a successful synthesis, Sherif (1951) wrote:

> Social psychology ... is still groping its way at the crossroads. Groping at the crossroads may be taken as a sign of vitality. A few decades ago, conditions were not even ripe for serious groping (p. 1).

Despite the hopes Sherif held for a meeting of the two approaches to social psychology, during the intervening period only limited cross-fertilization of the fruits of our labors has occurred. We suggest that the time is now ripe for some really serious groping!

Many published analyses of the two social psychologies exist, with recent work consisting of summaries of current research topics in the two disciplines (McMahon, 1983), suggestions of particular theories and research as the basis for a synthesis (Backman, 1983; Quinn, Robinson, & Balkwell, 1980; Stryker, 1983), and arguments for the institutional separation of the two social psychologies (Stryker, 1989). Here we present a general analysis of the current state of relations between the two social psychologies. First, we trace some barriers between the two social psychologies to differences in goals, as well as to historical, theoretical, and methodological differences. Second, we provide a social psychological explanation for some of the communication problems of the two social psychologies, based on intergroup relations theory and research. Last, we make practical suggestions as to how interchange between the two social psychologies can be furthered.

While we confine this analysis to the intersection of SSP and PSP, the relationship of the two social psychologies is a microcosm of the broader interaction between sociology and psychology. We feel that aspects of this analysis are applicable to the interactions of other social science disciplines as well.

Barriers Between the Two Social Psychologies

Negative stereotypes of each approach to social psychology held by members of the other discipline provide one barrier to communication between the two social psychologies. An examination of these stereotypes vividly demonstrates that traffic is not yet flowing smoothly through the intersection of SSP and PSP. What do we say about each other in the privacy of our offices and sometimes, in modified form, in print?

Psychological social psychologists are sometimes viewed as reformed rat-runners. They are thought to conduct artificial laboratory experiments in which they deceive college students for 50 minutes and then overgeneralize their findings to society at large. Sociologists may also believe PSP is unaware of the influence of the broader social structure on the individual behavior it studies.

On the other hand, psychologists subject to narrow graduate school training may not even be aware of the existence of SSP. Of those who are, many view SSP as symbolic interactionism, and characterize this school as being primarily interested in nuts and sluts. These sociologists are sometimes thought to become so immersed in their informants' lives that they lose their objectivity. They too are said to overgeneralize findings, from the one instance they have studied to all such groups. The psychologists who are aware of the personality and social structure perspective sometimes characterize it as having only one variable: SES. Psychologists tend to believe that the concern of the personality and social structure perspective with stratification and macro-level analyses makes it insensitive to psychological dynamics. (If you have ever wondered how the natural sciences can have such a negative view of the social sciences, consider that they may have access to what we say about each other!) These negative stereotypes can lead members of both disciplines to dismiss as unimportant the work conducted by members of the other discipline.

A second barrier to communication between the two social

psychologies consists of differences in the use of basic terms. This difference is not trivial, since it frustrates our good faith efforts to learn about each other's work by creating miscommunications of which we are often unaware. For instance, consider the term, "secondary analysis." In sociology, secondary analysis of data refers to the analysis of previously collected data. In psychology, it usually refers to internal analysis within main or interaction effects from an analysis of variance. There are many examples of this type that make members of each discipline think that social psychologists from the other discipline simply do not know what they are talking about.

To take another example, what could be a more common joint term than the term "norm?" The term "norm," as used by the psychologists Fishbein and Ajzen in their model of behavioral intentions (1975), refers to an individual's perception of the attitudes of significant others toward the action that is being contemplated. Shalom Schwartz, another psychological social psychologist, uses the term "norm" to signify an individual's own personal standards of conduct (1975). Neither of these uses of the term is consistent with usage by sociologists, who define "norm" in terms of a social consensus held about the appropriate conduct of the members of a social group. Examples of other terms that are used differently in the two disciplines include identity, empathy, assimilation, and scripts.

A third source of misunderstanding consists of misconceptions about the subject matter of the other discipline. For example, the sociologists House (1977) and Stryker (1977) state that PSP focuses on psychological processes within individuals, while the psychologist Blank (1978) defines SSP's focus as the relationship between individuals and social institutions, particularly behavior based on roles and norms. In general, sociologists appear to believe that PSP is exclusively concerned with intra-individual behavior; whereas, psychologists seem to believe that SSP is primarily concerned with social structure. These assumptions are incorrect. All sociological theories have some foundation in individual behavior (McPhail, 1981). Likewise, PSP often reflects a concern with social groups, norms, and roles, as well as with individuals (see, for example, Myers, 1990; Worchel & Cooper, 1983). The imperfect understanding of the subject matter of the other group leads the members of each discipline to believe little overlap exists between the two approaches.

We believe the critical difference between the two approaches lies not in their focus on intra- or extra-individual behavior, but in the goals of the two social psychologies. The title of George Herbert Mead's (1934) seminal work on social psychology may be used to explore the historical difference between the two social psychologies, since "mind," "self," and "society" are the words needed to discuss the triangular relationship between the two social psychologies and their parent disciplines.

Like other psychologists, researchers and theorists in PSP relate their knowledge of the self, or individuals, back to the mind, or psyche. They attempt to trace individual social behavior to its origins in the mind. While they are aware that the mind is dependent upon the society (Gergen & Davis, 1985), this fact is not given primary emphasis in PSP. On the other hand, researchers and theorists in SSP relate their knowledge of the self back to society, as do other sociologists. They attempt to trace individual social behavior to its origins in the structure of society. Since SSP is concerned with the reciprocal relationship of the self and society, it is also interested in the ways in which individuals influence society.

Due to the differences in their parent disciplines, we believe the goals of the two social psychologies differ. This difference in goals often manifests itself in the ways that empirical data are discussed by the two types of social psychologists. Researchers in PSP search their findings for their relevance to an understanding of the mind, whereas those in SSP search their findings for their relevance to an understanding of society. Thus the same idea, for instance, the finding that disadvantaged people are held responsible for their condition, is discussed in terms of its relevance for different universes of discourse. The psychologists relate it to individuals' needs to believe that the world is just (Lerner, 1980), while the sociologists relate it to the labeling of powerless members of society by the more powerful (Becker, 1963; Erikson, 1962).

We think the difference in goals is more important than the other differences that are typically cited--those between levels of analysis, methodologies, theoretical perspectives, and subject matter. Considerable overlap exists in all of these areas. However, methodological differences do exist, and contribute to the misunderstandings between the two social psychologies. PSP derives from an empirical tradition with roots in the natural sciences. PSP views the experimental approach as the fast track to truth. Given psychologists' reliance on deception in their research, sociologists sometimes appear to believe that the fast track to truth is laid on a foundation of lies. By contrast, symbolic interactionists derive from a tradition that has roots in observational methods. Some symbolic interactionists continue to use qualitative techniques such as participant observation, while the social structure and personality perspective of sociological social psychology favors large-scale survey research. Psychological social psychologists often distrust both the subjectivity of participant observation and the reanalysis of data collected for another purpose.

While mutual mistrust regarding techniques exists, and while observational, survey, and laboratory techniques may require different skills and different training to acquire these skills, no fundamental conflict exists between the methodologies of the two social psychologies. Use of one approach does not preclude the use of another. In fact, in an article published over a decade ago, social psychologists listed laboratory experimentation as the methodology for less than half their research, and sociological social psychologists listed various types of experimentation for nearly one-quarter of their research (Wilson & Schafer, 1978). This mixing of methodologies is probably even more prevalent today.

While SSP and PSP are characterized as differing considerably in theory, these differences are overdrawn. SSP is often mischaracterized as having one overriding theoretical perspective, symbolic interactionism, while PSP is often characterized as being atheoretical at best and merely faddish at worst (Ring, 1967). In fact, much social psychology undertaken by sociologists from the social structure and personality school and a great deal of PSP make use of the same major theories, such as exchange theory, role theory, social learning theory, and derivatives of Lewinian field theory. Also, both rely heavily on mini-theories that apply to single topic areas, such as theories of relationship formation and interpersonal attraction. Even within symbolic interactionism, the researchers deriving from the Chicago and Iowa traditions view this theory in rather different terms. Thus, we would argue that sociological theories are more differentiated than psychologists give them credit for being and psychologists are not as atheoretical as sociologists claim.

Next, we will consider a commonly cited, yet somewhat simple-minded, basis for differences. Sociologists and psychologists are said to have different substantive interests, with sociologists examining such topics as socialization, deviance, and collective behavior, and psychologists exploring such topics as conformity, aggression, and helping behavior. It should be obvious, however, that if divisions exist between the interests of researchers from the two disciplines, many of us have lost our way and strayed into the territory of the other discipline. Certainly one can argue that some areas of interest in SSP and PSP do not overlap. But it is easy to list a number of areas of common interest, including central topics in both disciplines such as the self, attitude formation and change, the relationship of thought to behavior, and intergroup relations.

However, even where SSP and PSP have a similar interest, their approaches to the topic have historically overlapped very little. For example, in the study of the self, psychologists have been concerned with such topics as self-schemata, self-disclosure, self-efficacy, and self-awareness. In contrast, sociologists have focused on the development of self-identity, self-esteem, and the influence of the social structure on the self.

Unfortunately, even when the same subtopic is studied in SSP and PSP--impression formation and self concept, for example--too few social psychologists of either persuasion are informed by work in the other discipline. The relationship between the work of Mead (1934) and Cooley (1902) concerning the influence of others on the development of the self and social comparison theory (Festinger, 1954) often goes unrecognized, as does the relevance of studies of self-awareness (Carver and Scheier, 1981; Wicklund, 1978) to work on face-to-face social interaction (Goffman, 1962, 1967, 1969). Similarly, the mutual relevance of the sociological work on the self to the psychological work on cognitive functioning is too often ignored (Kohn, 1989). One positive example can be found in Stryker's and other's analyses of the overlap between symbolic interactionism and attribution theory (Howard & Levinson, 1985; Stephan & Stephan, 1990; Stryker & Gottleib, 1981).

An Intergroup Relations Analysis of the Relations Between SSP and PSP

The estrangement of the two approaches goes beyond differences in goals, methods, and theories, although these differences do contribute to the problem. It often seems as though the two disciplines regard the acquisition of knowledge as a limited good; the more one discipline acquires, the less is available for the other discipline. This implicit notion may underlie some of the basic antagonisms that seem to exist between the two disciplines. Other similarly irrational reasons could be cited for the enmity that exists between the two disciplines. We will examine the relations between the two social psychologies as a case study of intergroup relations. We assume that psychologists and sociologists as social groups share the same tendencies toward intergroup perceptions as do other social groups. Just because we have been responsible for creating the knowledge does not mean we are immune to the biases that are a common part of intergroup relations.

In our own work we have used a model suggesting that antagonisms between groups stem from (1) prior intergroup relations--lack of contact or negative contact between groups; (2) prior intergroup cognitions--the lack of knowledge of the other groups, as well as stereotyping, prejudice, ethnocentrism, negative expectations, and perceptions of ingroup-outgroup differences (Stephan & Stephan, 1984, 1985); and (3) situational factors, such as amount of structure, type of interdependence between the groups, and group composition. We will examine the effect of each of these factors on each discipline's attitudes toward the other.

First we explore prior intergroup relations between members of the two social psychologies. Social psychological research suggests that lack of contact between groups leads to ignorance of the other group and that ignorance is a precursor of prejudice (Myrdal, 1944; Williams, 1947). Lack of contact has certainly contributed to the ignorance of the outgroup that exists across the two social psychologies. As a result, the goals, methods, and theories of each are often misunderstood or misrepresented by the other group. Previous negative contact, such as competition for scarce resources both within academic settings and for extramural funding, has also contributed to prejudice and the creation of negative stereotypes.

Next we focus on prior intergroup cognitions between the two social psychologies. Negative stereotypes and beliefs about outgroup members lead to negative intergroup relations because ingroup members expect negative behaviors from outgroup members (Stephan & Rosenfield, 1982; Stephan & Stephan, 1984). Recall the stereotypes regarding methodologies and theories of the other disciplines we presented earlier. Why are these stereotypes so extreme? A number of cognitive-processing biases contribute to stereotyping, among them perceptual assimilation and contrast. Assimilation is the perception of ingroups as more homogeneous than they actually are, while contrast is the perception of outgroups as more dissimilar than they actually are. Thus, real ingroup-outgroup differences are likely to be exaggerated due to perceptual assimilation and contrast effects (Miller & Brewer, 1984; Stephan, 1985). Because people tend to assume that members of outgroups are dissimilar to members of their own group, they anticipate disliking outgroup members and being disliked by them (Gonzales, Loney, LuKena, & Junghans, 1983). Stereotypes create expectancies and influence behavior in ways that create self-fulfilling prophecies. Thus, avoidance, disdain, and hostility among the members of one group can generate reciprocal negative responses from the other group.

A kind of disciplinary ethnocentrism is another cause of negative attitudes across disciplines (Hamilton, 1982; Hastie, Ostrom, Ebbesen, Wyer, Hamilton, & Carlston, 1980). Because our professions are such an important component of our identities, a natural tendency exists to view the ingroup in positive terms and, correspondingly, to view the outgroup in negative terms. We are often guilty of believing that our knowledge is better than that of the other group. Focusing on the differences between the two groups leads ingroup members to emphasize those differences on which they perceive the ingroup to be superior to the outgroup (Brewer, 1979). These selective perceptions enable the members of each group to view themselves positively. The processes of selective perception at work here are similar to those identified by the sociologist Rosenberg (1979) as contributing to positive self-esteem and those discussed by the psychologist Tajfel (1978) as contributing to the generic norm of ingroup-outgroup bias.

Cognitive biases such as the availability bias also contribute to these negative attitudes (Stephan, 1985; Tversky & Kahneman, 1973). The availability bias refers to the tendency for judgments to be biased by cognitions readily available in memory. Typically the most readily available information about members of other groups consists of negative or unusual characteristics. Some of the most memorable studies in both social psychologies are those that have raised the strongest concerns about ethics within and outside each discipline. Although few social psychologists ever conducted studies like those of Milgram (1974), his work on obedience is highly memorable and therefore is more readily available to characterize PSP than other experiments remembered less well. Likewise, Humphreys' studies of homosexuals in public restrooms (1975) provide an easily remembered instance of SSP.

In addition, there is a powerful tendency for people to seek out and remember information consistent with their expectations and to distort or forget inconsistent information (Stephan, 1985). Given the negative stereotypes and mistrust between the two groups, many of the expectancies are negative. Thus members of both groups are predisposed to perceive and retain information uncomplimentary to the other group, making it easier to retrieve this negative information from memory in the future.

Last, we turn to situational factors in intergroup relations. One influential situational factor is the type of interdependence existing between the groups. We have already noted that the previous contact between the two social psychologies is likely to have been in a competitive context, such as competition for extramural funding. It may be that the zero-sum game nature of our relationship to the acquisition of knowledge can be traced to the real zero-sum game that occurs for economic resources.

A second situational factor influencing intergroup relations is group size. When an unbalanced ratio exists between groups, the larger group may perceive itself as superior and may well have more power, while the smaller group is likely to resent the outgroup's presumption of its inferiority and fear the consequences of its relative powerlessness. Psychology's relative ignorance of the work in SSP may be a consequence of such a belief in its superiority, a belief which only the larger social psychology could possibly sustain. Concerns regarding the engulfment of SSP by PSP in any institutional merger (Stryker, 1989; this volume) demonstrate the threat inherent in low power associated with size.

Solutions to the Communication Problems of the Two Social Psychologies

Just as theoretical and empirical work in social psychology contributes to understanding the poor intergroup relations between sociologists and psychologists, it also can help us formulate solutions to the problem. We argue that in large part stereotyping and the various cognitive information biases are allowed to operate because they occur in a context of relative ignorance of the outgroup. If we increase our knowledge of the outgroup, we are likely to modify our stereotypes and to find it easier to override the influence of cognitive biases (Brislin & Pedersen, 1976; Stephan & Stephan, 1984; Triandis, 1975).

Previous research suggests two solutions to the problem of ignorance of the outgroup. First, information exchange between members of the groups can be used to solve intergroup ignorance and prejudice. Programs designed to reduce intergroup ignorance have been a topic of research for half a century. Overall, they have shown that exposure to accurate information about a group can successfully reduce prejudice (Stephan & Stephan, 1984).

Second, intergroup contact can be used as a means of changing intergroup relations. Social psychologists have identified a number of conditions that facilitate positive interpersonal relations. Intergroup contact is most successful in improving intergroup relations when it takes place in a cooperative setting among equal status participants and where institutional support exists for the interaction (Allport, 1954; Stephan, 1986; Williams, 1977). While past contact between members of the two social psychologies has frequently involved participants of equal status, often competition has pervaded the relations and institutional support for such interchanges has been lacking. A further condition for successful reduction of prejudice is contact with a substantial number of members of the outgroup. Multiple contacts allow for repeated disconfirmations of negative stereotypes to generalize from known outgroup members to the outgroup as a whole (Rothbart & John, 1985).

How might we increase knowledge of and positive contact between the two social psychologies? First, we can encourage desegregation of the practice of the two social psychologies. Joint academic endeavors of a variety of types could provide contact under near optimal conditions. We can broaden the gradual trend toward integration in the contents and editorial boards of social psychology journals. We can become acquainted with colleagues in the other discipline who are engaged in work related to ours by sending them reprints of our work. Joint exchange of information, joint research and jointly written and edited journal articles, grant proposals, and books might result. Interchanges of colloquia within universities, joint convention symposia, and a multidisciplinary newsletter could provide other avenues for informational and social exchange.

Second, we can make certain that the next generation of social psychologists is knowledgeable about the social psychology of both disciplines by requiring or strongly encouraging our students to take undergraduate and particularly graduate courses in each other's discipline, including methodology courses. If we augment our knowledge of the other discipline gained through contact by carefully reading the literature of the other discipline, we will be able to teach relevant material from the other discipline in our own courses, as well as reference literature from the other discipline in our journal articles and books.

Last, we can further relations between the two social psychologies in an important way by evaluating our colleagues favorably when they cross the disciplines, rather than penalizing them, as if they were illegal immigrants straying across a sacred border. With such changes freeways might be required to carry the traffic between the disciplines.

Some rapprochement between the two social psychologies has taken place in the last 20 years and the concerns and the interests of the two social psychologies are considerably closer than at any other time in their recent history. For instance, the focus in PSP on cognition has made the construction of meaning a central focus of PSP as well as SSP. This cognitive revolution began in the 1940's, with the "new look" in perception, continued in the 1960's with the emphasis on cognitive dissonance, and in the 1970's with attribution theory.

The 1980's zeitgeist of cognitive information processing has moved the concerns of PSP squarely in line with those of many in SSP. Psychologists, as well as sociologists, view humans as active agents, rather than primarily as products of the stimuli impinging on them. Both sociologists and psychologists acknowledge the importance of the meanings which people attribute to their own behavior and that of others in understanding social life.

The second dominant change in PSP in the last 20 years that has moved it closer to the concerns of SSP has been its emphasis on broad situational factors. While few of the individual studies are as well known as Rosenhan's (1973) studies of the situational influence on the judgment of mental illness, often the psychological social psychology of the last 20 years has demonstrated the power of the situation.

Along with this emphasis on situational factors has come a new concern with the joint influence of the individual and the situation and an emphasis on reciprocal influence among individuals. For example, recent studies have explored the role of others' expectancies on individuals' behaviors (Bodenhausen & Wyer, 1985; Skov & Sherman, 1986). Similarly, several perspectives within SSP, such as symbolic interactionism and labeling theory, have long been concerned with the others' influence on an individual's feelings and behaviors.

At the same time that these changes have been occurring in PSP, SSP has been moving closer to PSP. Quantitative methods have been used more and more commonly within SSP. The more quantitative Iowa school of symbolic interactionism has gained in prominence. Further, the sophistication of sociologists in quantitative analysis has broken new barriers for social psychologists in areas such as structural equation modeling. In addition, more sociologists are conducting laboratory or field experiments.

This convergence of the two disciplines provides stepping-stones to closer relations between SSP and PSP. Why should closer relations be pursued? First, to the extent that the approaches do have differing goals and methodologies, they provide complementary information regarding the same subject matter. Each of the views has weaknesses and strengths. As Newcomb (1951) wrote over 35 years ago:

> The major inadequacy of the psychological approach is that it has never really faced the implications of the psychologists' claim to study the organism in the environment, because it has been a bit naive concerning the full conditions of the (social system) under which the individual's perception of social behavior occurs. On the other hand, social psychology represented by the sociological approach is equally defective....It has taken human organisms as virtually empty receptacles into which culture is simply poured" (p. 5; see also Wrong, 1961).

Combining the approaches counterbalances the weaknesses of each approach with the strengths of the other.

Second, regardless of apparent differences of approach, the two views ultimately converge. Both sociologists and psychologists are actually working toward a theory of human behavior that accounts for individual behavior in its social context. Finally, together SSP and PSP share a concern with the subjective world of the individual that is a unique contribution of social psychology (Cartwright, 1979). Both perspectives emphasize the environment as perceived by the individual, rather than the actual environment.

Since the two social psychologies are converging, since we have always shared a common focus on cognitive interpretations of reality and subsequent behaviors based on these interpretations, and since we work from points of view that both converge and complement each other, we should set aside our old prejudices and make renewed efforts to learn about both social psychologies and to collaborate with each other.

What we advocate is akin to the pluralism without walls advocated by Andrew Greeley (1980). As he envisions it, this type of pluralism allows groups to retain their separate identities, but supports a free interchange of practices, ideas, and even membership between them. We think the two groups have much to offer one another. Both will be changed for the better in the process, but neither will be absorbed by the other. Our understanding of humans and of society will clearly broaden through our shared knowledge.

Acknowledgements. The authors thank Paul Secord and Clyde Hendrick for comments on earlier drafts of this manuscript.

References

Allport, C. W. (1954). *The nature of prejudice.* Reading, MA: Addison-Wesley.

Backman, C. W. (1983). Toward an interdisciplinary social psychology. In L. Berkowitz (Ed.), *Advances in experimental social psychology* (Vol. 16). New York: Academic Press.

Becker, H. S. (1963). *Outsiders.* New York: Free Press.

Blank, T. O. (1978). Two social psychologies: Is segregation inevitable or acceptable? *Personality and Social Psychology Bulletin, 4,* 553-556.

Bodenhausen, G. V., & Wyer, R. S., Jr. (1985). Effects of stereotypes on decision making and information-processing strategies. *Journal of Personality and Social Psychology Bulletin, 48,* 267-282.

Brewer, M. B. (1979). The role of ethnocentrism in intergroup conflict. In W. Austin & S. Worchel (Eds.), *The social psychology of intergroup relations.* Monterey, CA: Brooks/Cole.

Brislin, R. W., & Pederson, P. (1976). *Cross-cultural orientation programs.* New York: Gardner Press.

Cartwright, D. (1979). Contemporary social psychology in historical perspective. *Social Psychology Quarterly, 42,* 82-93.

Carver, C. S., & Scheier, M. F. (1981). *Attention and self-regulation.* New York: Springer-Verlag.

Cooley, C. H. (1902). *Human nature and the social order.* New York: Scribners.

Erikson, K. T. (1962). Notes on the sociology of deviance. *Social Problems, 9,* 307-314.

Festinger, L. (1954). A theory of social comparison processes. *Human Relations, 7,* 117-140.

Fishbein, M., & Ajzen, I. (1975). *Belief, attitude, intention, and behaviors: An introduction to theory and research.* Reading, MA: Addison-Wesley.

Gergen, K. J., & Davis, K. E. (1985). *The social construction of the person.* New York: Springer-Verlag.

Goffman, E. (1962). *The presentation of self in everyday life.* New York: Doubleday/Anchor.

Goffman, E. (1967). *Interaction ritual: Essays on face-to-face behavior.* New York: Doubleday/Anchor.

Goffman, E. (1969). *Strategic interaction.* New York: Ballentine.

Gonzales, M. H., Davis, J. M., Loney, G. L., LuKena, C. K., & Junghans, C. M. (1983). Interactional approach to interpersonal attraction. *Journal of Personality and Social Psychology, 43,* 702-709.

Greeley, A. (1980). School desegregation and ethnicity. In W. G. Stephan & J. R. Feagin (Eds.), *School desegregation: Past, present, and future.* New York: Plenum.

Hamilton, D. L. (Ed.). (1982). *Cognitive processes in stereotyping and intergroup behavior.* Hillsdale, NJ: Erlbaum.

Hastie, R., Ostrom, T. M., Ebbesen, E. B., Wyer, R. S., Jr., Hamilton, D. L., & Carlston, D. E. (1980). *Person memory: The cognitive basis of social perception.* Hillsdale, NJ: Erlbaum.

House, J. S. (1977). The three faces of social psychology. *Sociometry, 40,* 161-177.

Howard, J. A., & Levinson, R. (1985). The overdue courtship of attribution and labeling. *Social Psychology Quarterly, 48,* 192-202.

Humphreys, L. (1975). *Tearoom trade.* Chicago: Aldine.

Kohn, M. L. (1989). Social structure and personality: A quintessentially sociological approach to social psychology. *Social Forces, 68,* 26-33.

Lerner, M. J. (1980). *The belief in a just world: A fundamental delusion.* New York: Plenum.

McMahon, A. M. (1983). The two social psychologies: Postcrisis directions. *Annual Review of Sociology, 10,* 121-140.

McPhail, C. (1981). The problems and prospects of behavioral perspectives. *American Sociologist, 16,* 172-175.

Mead, G. H. (1934). *Mind, self, and society.* Chicago: University of Chicago Press.

Mischel, W. (1977). The interaction of person and situation. In D. Magnusson & N. S. Endler (Eds.), *Personality at the cross-roads: current issues in interactional psychology.* Hillsdale, NJ: Erlbaum.

Milgram, S. (1974). *Obedience to authority.* New York: Harper & Row.

Miller, N., & Brewer, M. B. (Eds.). (1984). *Groups in contact: The psychology of desegregation.* New York: Academic Press.

Myers, D. G. (1983). *Social psychology.* New York: McGraw Hill.

Myrdal, G. (1944). *An American dilemma.* New York: Harper.

Newcomb, T. M. (1951). Social psychological theory: Integrating individual and social approaches. In J. H. Rohrer and M. Sherif (Eds.), *Social psychology at the crossroads.* New York: Harper.

Quinn, C. O., Robinson, I. E., & Balkwell, J. W. (1980). A synthesis of two social psychologies. *Symbolic Interaction, 3,* 59-88.

Ring, K. (1967). Some sober questions about some frivolous values. *Journal of Experimental Social Psychology, 3,* 113-123.

Rohrer, J. M., & Sherif, M. (1951). *Social psychology at the crossroads.* New York: Harper.

Rosenberg, M. (1979). *Conceiving the self.* New York: Basic Books.

Rosenhan, D. L. (1973). On being sane in insane places. *Science, 173,* 250-258.

Rothbart, M., & John, O. P. (1985). Social categorization and behavioral episodes: A cognitive analysis of the effects of intergroup contact. *Journal of Social Issues, 41,* 81-104.

Schwartz, S. H. (1975). The justice of need and the activation of humanitarian norms. *Journal of Social Issues, 31,* 111-136.

Skov, R. B., & Sherman, S. J. (1986). Information-gathering processes: Diagnosticity, hypothesis-confirmatory strategies, and perceived hypothesis confirmation. *Journal of Experimental Social Psychology, 22,* 93-121.

Sherif, M. (1951). Introduction. In J. H. Rohrer and M. Sherif (Eds.), *Social psychology at the crossroads.* New York: Harper.

Stephan, C. W., & Stephan, W. G. (1990). *Two social psychologies* (2nd ed.). Belmont, CA: Wadsworth.

Stephan, W. G. (1985). Intergroup relations. In G. Lindzey and E. Aronson (Eds.), *Handbook of social psychology* (3rd ed.). New York: Random House.
Stephan, W. G. (1986). The effects of school desegregation: An evaluation 30 years after *Brown*. In M. Saks & L. Saxe (Eds.), *Advances in applied social psychology*. New York: Erlbaum.
Stephan, W. G., & Rosenfield, D. (1982). Racial and ethnic stereotypes. In A. G. Miller (Ed.), *In the eye of the beholder*. New York: Praeger.
Stephan, W. G., & Stephan, C. W. (1984). The role of ignorance in intergroup relations. In N. Miller and M. B. Brewer (Eds.), *Desegregation: Groups in contact*. New York: Academic Press.
Stephan, W. G., & Stephan, C. W. (1985). Intergroup anxiety. *Journal of Social Issues*, *41*, 157-175.
Stryker, S. (1977). Developments in two social psychologies: Toward an appreciation of mutual relevance. *Sociometry*, *40*, 145-160.
Stryker, S. (1983). Social psychology from the standpoint of a structural symbolic interactionist: Toward an interdisciplinary social psychology. In L. Berkowitz (Ed.), *Advances in experimental social psychology* (Vol. 16). New York: Academic Press.
Stryker, S. (1989). The two social psychologies: Additional thoughts. *Social Forces*, *68*, 45-54.
Stryker, S., & Gottlieb, A. (1981). Attribution theory and symbolic interactionism: A comparison. In J. H. Harvey, W. Ickes, and R. E. Kidd (Eds.), *New directions in attribution research* (Vol. 3). Hillsdale, NJ: Erlbaum.
Tajfel, H. (1978). *Differentiation between social groups*. London: Academic Press
Triandis, H. C. (1975). Culture training, cognitive complexity, and interpersonal attitudes. In R. Brislin, S. Bouchner, and W. Lonner (Eds.), *Cross-cultural perspectives on learning*. Beverly Hills, CA: Sage.
Tversky, A., & Kahneman, D. (1973). Availability: A heuristic for judging frequency and probability. *Cognitive Psychology*, *5*, 207-232.
Wicklund, R. A. (1978). Objective self-awareness. In L. Berkowitz (Ed.), *Cognitive theories in social psychology*. New York: Academic Press.
Williams, R. M., Jr. (1947). *The reduction of intergroup tensions: A survey of research on problems of ethnic, racial, and religious group relations*. New York Social Science Research Council.
Williams, R. M., Jr. (1977). *Mutual accommodation: Ethnic conflict and cooperation*. Minneapolis: University of Minnesota Press.
Wilson, D. W., & Schafer, R. B. (1978). Is social psychology interdisciplinary? *Personality and Social Psychology Bulletin*, *4*, 548-552.
Worchel, S., & Cooper, J. (1983). *Understanding social psychology* (3rd ed.). Homewood, IL: Dorsey.
Wrong, D. (1961). The oversocialized conception of man in modern society. *American Sociological Review*, *26*, 183-193.

4
Sociology, Psychology and Social Psychology (and Social Science)

James S. House

A little over a decade ago, I wrote one of the numerous papers of the 1970s analyzing the perceived "crisis" of social psychology of that time (House, 1977). My particular diagnosis of that crisis was that it reflected the division of social psychology into three increasingly isolated domains or faces: (1) psychological social psychology, (2) symbolic interactionism, and (3) what I termed psychological sociology or what is more often labelled as the study of social structure and personality. I saw the solution to the crisis in greater unification of, or at least interchange between, the three faces and their disparate substantive and methodological concerns, though I had only tentative ideas on how that might be achieved, and was uncertain that it could be. Much of what I wrote ten years ago remains valid in my view, but I also have revised or extended my thinking on some issues.

That a decade later we are still discussing the unification of social psychology can be viewed both negatively and positively. The unification of social psychology is still problematic and the field is still somewhat in crisis. Many of the problems evident in the 1970s are still with us, and I will argue have now generalized, contributing to a current broader malaise in social science. Yet we can also see positive developments in social psychology and its parent disciplines of sociology and psychology, which give us hope that past and current crises may yet be transcended.

This chapter addresses a number of issues. First, what is social psychology? If we are going to increase the unity of social psychology we need to understand what it is that we seek to unify. Second, why is the unity of social psychology problematic; that is, in what ways does social psychology lack unity and why do we want to or need to increase this unity? Third, what would an appropriately unified social psychology look like and how might we achieve greater unification?

Fourth and finally, what have we accomplished over the past decade toward unifying social psychology, and what remains to be attained?

What Is Social Psychology?

To unify social psychology, we must know what social psychology is, in all its disparate parts. If we define the nature of the field differently, we will have very different conceptions of what a unified social psychology should look like, and how close the current approximation is to our ideal. Social psychologists may feel quite different needs to further unify social psychology, because some definitions of social psychology are no more than parts of the total field as others define it.
the true "final science" which Auguste Comte sought to create toward the end of his life (Allport, 1968:6-10)--a combination of sociology,

My conception of social psychology is quite broad, approximating psychology, and biology, which are the three basic sciences of individual behavior and social life. In the long run, we must integrate biological concerns with the concerns of social psychology and the

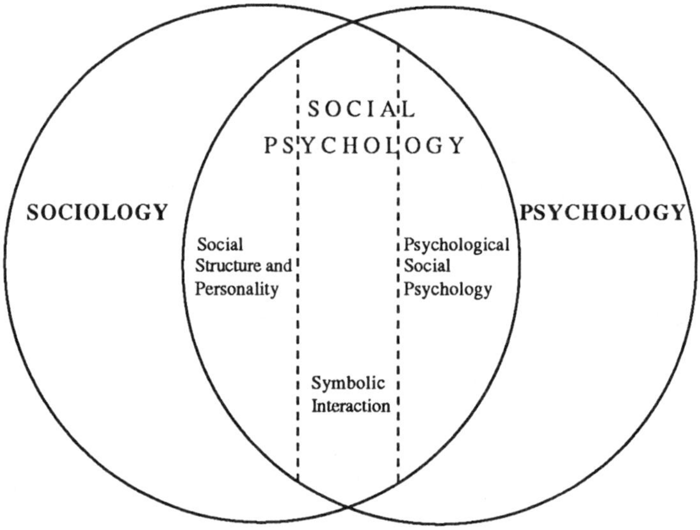

FIGURE 1. Social Psychology as the Intersection of Sociology and Psychology

other social sciences, as has already begun to be done in areas such as sociobiology and psychophysiology. I focus here, however, only on sociology, psychology and their intersection, social psychology. Psychology is the science of *individual* behavior and mental functioning; sociology is the science of the structure and functioning, or *social organization*, of social groups or collectivities. Social psychology is the intersection of these two fields, graphically

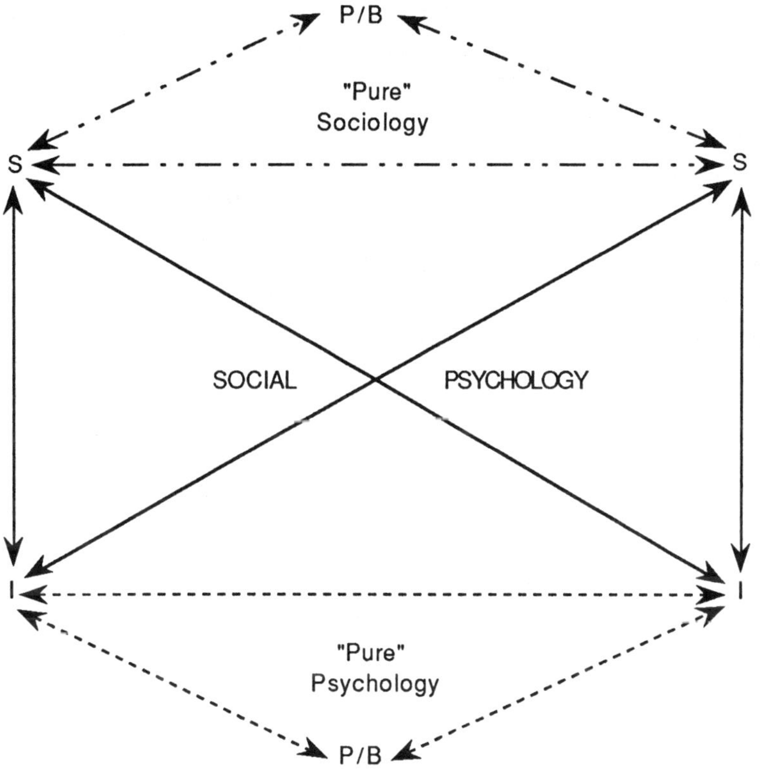

Key: S = Property of Social Organization
I = Property of Individual
P/B = Property of Physical/Biological Environment

FIGURE 2. Social Psychology as the Study of Relations Between Properties of Social Organizaions and of Individuals

represented in Figure 1, just as biochemistry or biophysics represents the intersection of biology with chemistry or physics.

It is difficult to study individuals totally apart from their social context, or to study social organizations without recognizing that all patterns of social life are produced by sets of individual actors. There are, however, as indicated in Figure 2, many areas of study which are purely sociological (dotted arrows in Figure 2) in that they involve relationships among properties of organizations or collectivities (or between these and their physical or biological environments), and others which are purely psychological (dashed arrows in Figure 2) in that they involve relationships among properties of individuals (or between these and the physical or biological environment). Social psychology has as its province relationships between properties of groups, or organizations, and properties of individuals (solid arrows in Figure 2).

A general or fully unified social psychology will encompass all relationships of this last type, but the number of such relationships is almost infinite, and their nature quite disparate because properties of both individuals and of social organizations are numerous and varied. Indeed, the major branches or faces of social psychology largely differ in the number and types of properties of individuals and social organizations on which they focus, as well as in the methods they use. Psychological social psychology focuses on how a broad array of properties of individuals are influenced by any social stimuli, usually the actual or implied presence or action of one or a few individuals (cf. Allport, 1968:3; Jones & Gerard, 1967). Thus, as indicated in Figure 1 its concerns lie close to the center of psychology, as does its emphasis on experimental method. Analogously, the concerns of the social structure and personality face of sociological social psychology focus on the relation of macroscopic properties of social organization (e.g., "class," "modernization," "urbanicity," etc.) to a limited range of individual attributes, using largely survey methods (House, 1981), thus lying close to the center of the discipline of sociology in terms of both substance and methods (again, see Figure 1). With its focus on studying social interaction and the microscopic properties of social situations using largely qualitative observational methods, symbolic interactionism is more on the fringe of both sociology and psychology.

Both Figures 1 and 2 suggest that the field of social psychology is very broad, at least as broad as either parent discipline. This broad field has several key aspects. First, it provides a meta-theoretical framework for thinking about individual behavior and social organization as joint functions of properties of the individual and of the social situation. This general perspective is fundamental to any unified social psychology, yet is only minimally adhered to in the most psychological or social variants of social psychology. Such a perspective must be shared among all members of a truly unified social psychology.

Second, the field of social psychology is comprised of different major substantive/theoretical and methodological approaches, such as the three faces denoted in Figure 1. These different faces or branches of social psychology can potentially be unified because they all share the general meta-theoretical focus on simultaneously considering properties of individuals and of social organizations, and because all can be used to study and understand each of the specific problems or phenomena which are the substantive content of social psychology at any point in time.

Finally, the field of social psychology is comprised at any one time of a series of specific areas of theory and research (e.g., dissonance or attribution theory, reference groups, group dynamics, interpersonal attraction, intergroup relations, etc.). It is important to recognize that these areas of theory and research will change with time and hence cannot be used to define the field. The unity of the field will be manifest in its ability to utilize a common general meta-theoretical perspective and the broad theoretical and methodological perspectives of each face to advance understanding of any specific problem. Indeed, as will become clearer below, I continue to believe that a broad and sustained focus on understanding specific social phenomena or problems is the sine qua non for unifying social psychology.

Why Should We Unify Social Psychology?

The perceived "crisis" of social psychology of the late 1960s and 1970s emerged at the end of a period of several decades of explosive and exciting growth in both the size of the field and the quality of its theory and research. As Cartwright (1979) has cogently argued, World War II was the single greatest stimulant to the growth and development of social psychology, and the social sciences more generally. For social psychology, the period from the 1930s to the 1960s was one of theoretical and methodological innovation, practical utilization, and considerable unity and integration within and across disciplinary boundaries. Social psychologists from sociology and psychology collaborated with each other and with other social scientists using surveys, experiments, and naturalistic observation to study a wide range of problems and phenomena of civilian and military life. These topics included communication and influence at the level of small groups and mass societies, group dynamics and performance, intergroup relations, among others (e.g., the landmark American Soldier studies of Stouffer et al., 1949-50). During its growth and success, social psychology was in the vanguard of the progress of the social sciences.

The very growth and success of the field became a source of problems, however, by promoting a growing specialization and fractionation of social psychology. Social psychologists in sociology and psychology grew apart from each other and closer to their colleagues in other areas of the parent discipline--producing in psychology a narrowing of substantive and methodological interests toward the study of more psychological and less social topics almost exclusively with experimental methods (cf. Katz, 1972; McGuire, 1973; Personality and Social Psychology Bulletin, 1976a, 1976b), and in sociology a dissipation of social psychology as social psychological concerns became amalgamated, and often left implicit, in the more general sociology of specific areas such as politics, medicine, family, race relations, mass communication, etc. (Liska, 1977). Many, including myself, perceived that the emergent crisis of social psychology could be solved only by a return toward the more unified state from which social psychology had just emerged.

Before accepting this prescription, however, we need to ask why and how greater unification constitutes at least a partial solution to the perceived crisis of social psychology? Is a desire to unify social psychology just a form of nostalgia for a bygone era when our field was smaller and its reputation and prospects seemingly brighter? Or is it merely a perceptual or aesthetic preference for wholeness as opposed to segmentation? I think the answer on both counts is no.

We seek greater unity in social psychology because the growing specialization and fractionation of the field has impeded its ability to accomplish its basic purpose--to understand, explain, and predict consequential real-life social phenomena and problems. Specialization is a natural and valuable process in the development of science. Two undesirable tendencies are, however, byproducts of specialization which must be opposed in some way by countervailing forces. First, specialization produces strong tendencies for scientists to learn more and more about less and less, and to have colleagues with whom they can collaborate, interact and communicate more and more about less and less. Second, increasing amounts of time and energy are spent in asserting the value and priority of the work of one's own subfield and often criticizing or denigrating the value of other subfields. This latter tendency is particularly pronounced along broad theoretical or methodological lines. For example, experimentation (or qualitative observation) (or survey research) is the only valid method of science; or cognitive processes, (or symbolic interaction) (or macro-micro relationships) are the core of the field, and all else peripheral. By the late 1960s, many social psychologists had become increasingly preoccupied with pursuing and protecting their own particular theories and methods rather than with understanding, explaining, and predicting major real life social phenomena and problems.

The perception of crisis in social psychology in the 1970s resulted fundamentally, then, not from nostalgia or purely aesthetic preferences for a more wholistic vision of social psychology, but from a sense that the field was becoming less successful in its major scientific purposes, even as it seemed to prosper quantitatively. Perhaps because its disciplinary divisions made its fractionation more manifest, social psychology was in the vanguard of the social sciences in recognizing a problem which has become increasingly apparent in other fields or disciplines of social science during the 1980s. Sociology, for example, has been characterized over the past decade by increasing feelings of malaise. The basis of this malaise is often, quite correctly I think, seen to lie in a growing tendency of sociologists to advocate particular theories or methods for their own sake rather than for their ability to significantly advance our understanding of fundamental social phenomena or problems (cf. Coser, 1975; Collins, 1986).

Randall Collins (1986), for example, sees a "crisis in sociological knowledge" due to the tendency of both scientific and humanistic sociology to deviate increasingly from the fundamental scientific ideal of understanding consequential aspects of social reality:

> What makes a science livingand vital is...that it is an intellectual vision, an accurate grasp of what at least crucial aspects of the world "out there" are really like. It is because Newton, or Einstein, or Darwin was really onto something that it was possible for his paradigms to set puzzles for subsequent research...This broad conception of science...is explicitly cumulative and integrating (Collins, 1986:1341-1345).

How Should We Unify Social Psychology?

My 1977 paper devoted almost 12 pages to describing how and why social psychology had become fractionated into three increasingly separate faces, and barely two pages to considering how it might become more unified. My basic prescription was to recapture one of the crucial characteristics of social psychology (and other social sciences) during and after World War II, which is also crucial to Collins' and my conception of any well-functioning science. Specifically, social psychologists (and other social scientists) collectively focused their work during World War II and for much of the succeeding two decades on *understanding, explaining, and predicting specific social phenomena or problems, all of which were seen as having some ultimate applied value* (cf. House, 1977). I continue to believe that a similar focus of social psychology today on consequential social phenomena or problems is essential to any effort to unify the field and hence improve the quality of its science. When scientists of any type focus their efforts on understanding, explaining, or predicting consequential phenomena or problems in the real world, they immediately become more eclectic and catholic in their orientation. Any concept, theory, or method that improves our ability to understand, explain or predict the social phenomenon or problem in question is worth learning about and using. Thus, a given researcher will tend to draw on a wider range of theory and methods and researchers from disparate backgrounds have a basis for communicating and collaborating in pursuit of a common good. Stanley Schachter has offered a similar prescription for doing high quality and innovative social psychology:

> ...if I were forced to give advice, I'd say get problem-oriented, follow your nose and go where the problems lead you. Then if something opens up that's interesting and that requires techniques and knowledge with which you're unfamiliar, learn them (quoted in Evans, 1976:168).

Though I cannot claim expertise in these areas, I perceive that dynamic areas of the natural sciences such as molecular biology or computer and information science share this property of problem-focus leading to creative cumulations and syntheses of theories and/or methods from diverse subfields or disciplines. I suggest below that some of the most dynamic areas of social psychology today share this property.

The problem of achieving greater unification of social psychology through greater problem-focus is a social and social psychological problem rather than a purely individual one. We will not unify social psychology within the heads of individuals, for the scope of theory and methods in the field is simply too broad for any individual to master. Individuals must have a sufficient breadth of knowledge and perspective to relate to and appreciate disparate approaches to common problems, but the integrative and unifying forces in social psychology must be primarily structural in nature. I think two sets of structures are particularly important--those in which individual social psychologists are educated and trained and those which shape the nature of their scientific activities.

Interdisciplinary and Problem-focused Training. Formal and informal structures of interdisciplinary graduate education and research in many universities constituted major bases of the relative unity of social psychology in the post-World War II period. All of the formal programs, and many of the informal structures, of interdisciplinary graduate training were lost in the late 1960s and 1970s as academic institutions became more disciplinary in orientation. We neither can easily nor should recreate the formal interdisciplinary graduate program structures. Stryker (1989) has cogently argued that while structures and processes to increase the integration of psychological and sociological social psychology are desirable and needed, full institutional unification would be undesirable. Psychological and sociological social psychologists are likely to have the most to offer each other if they are firmly grounded in their core disciplines (see Kohn, 1989 for a compelling argument on the need for social psychology to be more sociological). Similarly, each discipline benefits from having within it social psychologists who make psychology more social and sociology more psychological. Nevertheless, we can and should also foster structures and processes which will create a more unified and interdisciplinary foundation for social psychology even while retaining separate social psychology programs within both psychology and sociology departments.

If social psychology is the intersection of sociology and psychology, then it is impossible for an individual to be a competent social psychologist without some grounding in both disciplines, just as a biochemist must be grounded in both biology and chemistry. No one can seriously study one of the natural sciences without also being required to master at least the basic elements of all the others, and to study one of the interdisciplinary natural sciences requires substantial grounding in both parent disciplines. A major deficiency of current training in social psychology and the social sciences more generally, is that we do not require a similarly broad foundation of our students. Sociology or psychology can be studied without even being exposed to the full range of a single discipline, much less to have acquired a foundation in other disciplines of social science. Nor is training within social science disciplines as coherent and cumulative as it could be. This is one source of the current difficulties of the social sciences.

To allow social psychologists to be trained without a coherent and cumulative foundation in both of the parent disciplines is virtually to preclude the possibility of a unified social psychology. To define social psychology as a field of sociology or of psychology, and to allow training to be confined to that discipline will ultimately lead to the dissipation and disappearance of the field, as Steiner (1986) feels is happening to social psychology in psychology and Liska (1977) argues has already occurred in sociology. No one can be equally grounded, much less expert in both fields. But we must require that, through a combination of graduate and undergraduate training, professional social psychologists be grounded in the basic elements of both parent disciplines, in an interdisciplinary conception of the field, and in the various substantive and methodological faces of social psychology.

This foundation of undergraduate and graduate education must be reinforced and given more concrete expression at more advanced stages of training through seminars and research experience that are heavily problem-focused. Problem-focused research experiences will give students a chance to apply the broad foundation they have learned, and to acquire new substantive and methodological knowledge as needed. Social psychologists will still specialize in subareas of the larger field, and some will specialize in particular theoretical and methodological approaches, but all will see what they are doing in the context of a broader, interdisciplinary, problem-focused field.

Interdisciplinary, Problem-Focused Professional Structures. A basic truism of social psychology is that personal dispositions acquired at one stage of education, socialization, or development persist only if they are reinforced by the subsequent social environment (e.g., Newcomb et al., 1967). This requires that the structures in which we live our professional lives support the notion of an interdisciplinary, problem-focused social psychology. This can be achieved by building in and even mandating an interdisciplinary, problem-focused orientation even in structures which are largely the creature of a single discipline, and also building some explicitly interdisciplinary structures. The professional meetings and journals of social psychologists are largely within the province of the disciplinary associations such as ASA and APA. Yet there is no reason that we cannot foster cross-disciplinary memberships and participation in the meetings and activities of the social psychology sections of ASA and APA and on the editorial boards and pages of the major journals--the *Social Psychology Quarterly* (SPQ) and the *Journal of Personality and Social Psychology* (JPSP). We may also want to consider the need for one or more explicitly interdisciplinary associations or journals of social psychology. (See Stryker, 1989 for some similar and related ideas.)

We should similarly seek to foster interdisciplinary orientations and structures within the organizations that have most influence on our professional lives--research funding agencies, universities, and other employers. Within universities, truly interdisciplinary centers or institutes of research and scholarship in social science are one such mechanism which complements the disciplinary orientation of departments. The review processes and funding mechanisms of research funding agencies should also be organized to promote both interdisciplinary, problem-focused research as well as primarily disciplinary research. Such structures can be the necessary complement and countervailing force to the disciplinary departments and associations.

In sum, it is not enough to simply exhort social psychology to become more problem-focused and unified as I and others did in the 1970s. We need to begin to develop systematic policies and structures which encourage and facilitate unified and problem-focused research, thus countering the pressures toward specification and fractionation created by the nature of social psychology as the intersection of two traditional academic disciplines, and the sheer growth of social psychology and its parent disciplines. These suggestions are not novel but represent the extension of ongoing trends, suggesting that social psychology is emerging from the crisis of the 1970s and slowly becoming more unified. Our goal should be to solidify and strengthen these trends.

Are We Making Progress In Unifying Social Psychology?

Not long ago, Ivan Steiner (1986) looked back on things he had written and said in the early 1970s about the state of social psychology, especially the place of the study of group dynamics in social psychology (by "social psychology" he refers essentially to psychological social psychology). Earlier Steiner (1974) had argued that the decline of group dynamics and the increasingly experimental and psychological focus of psychological social psychology in the early 1970s was a temporary aberration, soon to be replaced by a resurgent emphasis on social and group phenomena. In contrast, Steiner (1986) reports that a colleague, Seymour Berger, predicted that "by the 1990s social psychology would be hard to find anywhere; it would have been assimilated into other areas of psychology such as learning, motivation, and cognition." Steiner (1986:279-286) concludes that his colleague's predictions have proven more accurate than his own, and he renews the call for a more unified social psychology:

> Substantively and methodologically the contemporary version of social psychology so thoroughly overlaps other areas of psychology that it has little claim to distinctiveness, and social psychology has failed to provoke a very supportive intellectual environment for the study of groups...It is not my contention that individualistic social psychology should somehow be suppressed and replaced by a more "groupy" variety. But individualistic social psychology should be combined and coordinated with an almost nonexistent psychology of *collective* behavior, without which it often provides a distorted picture of the individual's functioning (Steiner, 1986:285).

While I would agree that the mainstream of psychological social psychology remains very cognitive and experimental, and that the study of small groups has been largely dormant in all branches of social psychology, I come away from a period of reading and thinking about the state of unification in social psychology more sanguine and optimistic than Steiner seems to be, or than I thought I would be when I started. Steiner's pessimism stems in a large part from his own lack of knowledge or consideration of developments in sociological social psychology, which are part of the source of my optimism, but I am also more sanguine about developments in psychological social psychology and the prospects for greater unity in the total field of social psychology.

The increased vitality of the Social Psychology Section of ASA over the past decade, based on active involvement of representatives of all three faces of social psychology, has been one source of progress. The programs and awards and other activities of the Section have fostered increased appreciation of, and interaction among, different branches of the field. A broadening of content has also been evident in the *Social Psychology Quarterly*. The mainstream of sociology has also become more concerned with, and accepting of explicitly social psychological analysis, although the term social psychological is often still avoided in favor of the term microsociology and micro-macro relations (e.g., Coleman, 1986; Collins, 1986). On the other hand, it is not clear as we enter the 1990s that this progress is being fully sustained (Stryker, 1989).

Intellectually, Sheldon Stryker and Carl Backman and others have built bridges between psychological and sociological social psychology (Stryker, 1983; Backman, 1983), and Stryker (1985) and Turner (1978; 1988) have also tried to integrate symbolic interactionism with the more structural concerns of social structure and personality approach and some aspects of psychological social psychology as well. Stephan and Stephan (1986) have produced the first textbook that explicitly addresses the need for a social psychology which bridges psychological and sociological concerns.

Within psychological social psychology there has also been more change from the 1970s than Steiner recognizes. The mainstream is still cognitive and experimental, but the river of social psychology is broader and the mainstream a smaller part of the whole. Most striking has been the transformation of the *Journal of Personality and Social Psychology* (JPSP). The editorship of Anthony G. Greenwald provided shock treatment to a growing pattern of increasingly narrow one-shot experimental studies, and the reverberations produced a new format in which "attitudes and social cognition" became only one section of JPSP with "interpersonal relations and group processes" and "personality processes and individual differences" as co-equal members of a new troika. The result has been increased representation of both quantitative nonexperimental methods and a wide range of substantive concerns which are simultaneously more social and applied in nature. We have yet to see the real representation of either face of sociological social psychology in the professional activities and journals of psychological social psychology, but the time may be ripe for such representation.

Most heartening for me has been the emergence into the mainstream of all faces of social psychology, and of the parent disciplines of sociology and psychology, of major lines of research focused on understanding, explaining, and predicting significant social phenomena and problems rather than on merely extending existing lines of social psychological theory and methods. Among the most prominent examples are social psychological analyses of (1) health and illness; (2) sex and gender; (3) aging; (4) cognition and emotions; (5) race and ethnicity; and (6) deviance and law. This is a selective list. Rodin (1985) offers other examples, and Stryker (1989) and Rosenberg (1989) show that "the self" has become a more theoretical integrative focus for both psychological and sociological social psychologists.

Rodin (1985) has demonstrated the vitality of problem-focused applied research, which emerged in her view partially in response to the "crisis" in social psychology in the 1970s, and has documented its ability not only to test existing social psychological theory but also to stimulate new conceptual and theoretical developments. I have been impressed with the extent to which social psychologists from diverse backgrounds and perspectives have come first to work on common problems, second to utilize concepts and methods from other branches of social psychology, and increasingly to actually collaborate in research. In the health area, which I know best, psychological social psychologists such as David Glass, Karen Matthews, Judith Rodin, Jerome Singer, Shelley Taylor, and Camille Wortman who were originally trained in cognitive and experimental approaches, have come to utilize a broad array of non-experimental methods and more social theories and concepts in their work.

Similarly, sociological social psychologists out of the social structure and personality tradition, such as John Clausen, Ronald Kessler, Leonard Pearlin, David Mechanic, Peggy Thoits, myself, and others have been attracted toward more explicit and sophisticated psychological theory and greater use of longitudinal and quasi-experimental methods. Our own research group at Michigan now includes sociologists, psychologists, and social epidemiologists in active collaboration. Symbolic interactionism also has a long tradition of work in the health area, most notably in the work of Murray Strauss, Fred Davis, and colleagues at the University of California San Francisco Medical Center. Differences in methodological approach have slowed the integration of symbolic interactionist work with the other traditions, but evidence of convergence is beginning to appear in the work of some younger scholars (e.g., Anspach, forthcoming). Similar trends are occurring in other problem areas besides health.

In sum, we by no means have as unified a social psychology as we need. The disciplinary organization of science and academia, coupled with the forces of growth and specialization, maintain continuing pressures toward fractionation in social psychology and the social sciences more generally. The crisis of the 1970s has, however, led to changes in the direction of unification, changes which need to be reinforced and extended. In this regard social psychology may be again providing an example for other social sciences for ways of integrating disparate methodological and theoretical approaches to produce a more satisfactory science of individual behavior and social life. Our ability to achieve a more unified and problem-focused approach in social psychology, and in the social sciences more broadly, will be critical to their future support and development within the academic and scientific communities and the larger society.

Acknowledgements. I am indebted to Wendy Fisher House, Daniel Katz and Joseph Veroff for helpful comments on an earlier draft.

References

Allport, G. (1968). The historical background of modern social psychology. In G. Lindzey & E. Aronson (Eds.), *Handbook of social psychology* (2nd ed.) (Vol. 1). Reading, MA: Addison-Wesley.

Anspach, R. (in press). *Life and death decisions in neonatal intensive care: A study in the sociology of knowledge.* Berkeley: University of California Press.

Backman, C. W. (1983). Toward an interdisciplinary social psychology. In L. Berkowitz (Ed.), *Advances in experimental social psychology* (Vol. 16) (pp. 220-262). Orlando, FL: Academic Press.

Cartwright, D. (1979). Contemporary social psychology in historical perspective. *Social Psychology Quarterly*, *42*, 82-93.

Coleman, J. S. (1986). Social theory, social research and a theory of social action. *American Jouranl of Sociology*, *91*, 1309-1335.

Collins, R. (1986). Is 1980s sociology in the doldrums? *American Journal of Sociology*, *91*, 1336-1355.

Coser, L. (1975). Two methods in search of a substance. *American Sociological Review*, *40*, 691-700.

Evans, R. I. (1976). *The making of social psychology: Discussions with creative contributors.* New York: Knopf.

House, J. S. (1977). The three faces of social psychology. *Sociometry*, *40*, 161-177.

House, J. S. (1981). Social structure and personality. In M. Rosenberg & R. Turner (Eds.), *Sociological perspectives on social psychology* (pp. 421-452). New York: Basic Books.

Jones, E. E., & Gerard, H. B. (1967). *Foundation of social psychology.* New York: Wiley.

Katz, D. (1972). Some final considerations about experimentation in social psychology. In C. G. McClintock (Ed.), *Experimental social psychology* (pp. 549-561). New York: Holt, Rinehart and Winston.

Kohn, M. L. (1989). Social structure and personality: A quintessentially sociological approach to social psychology. *Social Forces*, *68*, 26-33.

Liska, A. E. (1977). The dissipation of sociological social psychology. *American Sociologist*, *12*, 2-8.

McGuire, W. J. (1973). The yin and yang of progress in social psychology. Seven koan. *Journal of Personality and Social Psychology*, *26*, 446-456.

Newcomb, T. M., Koenig, K. E., Flacks, R., & Warwick, D.P. (1967). *Persistence and change: Bennington College and its sutdents after 25 years.* New York: Wiley.

Personality and Social Psychology Bulletin. (1976a). (Vol. 2). Washington, D.C.: Society for Personality and Social Psychology.

Personality and Social Psychology Bulletin. (1976b). (Vol. 2). Washington, D.C.: Society for Personality and Social Psychology.

Rodin, J. (1985). Applied social psychology. In G. Lindzey & E. Aronson, *Handbook of social psychology* (pp. 805-882). New York: Random House.

Rosenberg, M. (1989). Self-concept research: A historical overview. *Social Forces*, *68*, 34-44.

Steiner, I. D. (1974). Whatever happened to the group in social psychology? *Journal of Experimental Social Psychology*, *10*, 94-108.
Steiner, I. D. (1986). Paradigms and groups. In L. Berkowitz (Ed.), *Advances in experimental social psychology* (Vol. 19) (pp. 251-289). Orlando, FL: Academic Press.
Stephan, C. W. & Stephan, W. G. (1986). *Two social psychologies: An integrative approach*. Homewood, Ill: The Dorsey Press.
Stouffer, S. A. et al. (1949-1950). *Studies in social psychology in World War II*. (Vols. 1-4). Princeton, NJ: Princeton University Press.
Stryker, S. (1983). Social psychology from the standpoint of a structural symbolic interactionism: Toward an interdisciplinary social psychology. In L. Berkowitz (Ed.), *Advances in experimental social psychology* (Vol. 16) (pp. 181-218). Orlando, FL: Academic Press.
Stryker, S. (1985). Symbolic interaction and role theory. In G. Lindzey & E. Aronson (Eds.), *Handbook of social psychology* (Vol. 1) (pp. 311-378). New York: Random House.
Stryker, S. (1989). The two psychologies: Additional thoughts. *Social Forces*, *68*, 45-54.
Turner, R. H. (1978). The role and the person. *American Journal of Sociology*, *84*, 1-23.
Turner, R. H. (1988). Personality in society: Social psychology's contribution to sociology. *Social Psychology Quarterly*, *51*, 1-10.

5
Interdisciplinary Social Psychology: Prospects and Problems

Carl W. Backman

In recent years there have appeared numerous signs of increasing convergence between the sociological and psychological traditions in social psychology. The latest edition of *The Handbook of Social Psychology* (Lindzey & Aronson, 1985) includes considerably more references to sociological materials than previous editions. This, of course, might be expected for the new chapter on symbolic interaction and role theory prepared by two sociologists, Stryker and Statham. The same can be said for the new chapters on survey methods and social deviance by sociologists. But one may note considerable sociological input in the chapters prepared by psychologists on socialization in adulthood and on sex roles. Some of the chapters in the latest edition covering topics dealt with in the earlier editions also reflect increased sociological input. The chapter on organizations, again by a sociologist, contains many sociological references, and the chapter by a psychologist on language has a definite sociolinguistic flavor, in contrast to the chapter on psycholinguistics in the second edition of the *Handbook.*

Another sign has been the publication in recent years of two introductory social psychology texts having a clear interdisciplinary-orientation, one by the Stephans (1985) and the other by Michener, De Lamater and Schwartz (1986).

Several years ago, both Stryker (1983) and I (Backman, 1983) suggested that this growing convergence was largely due to shifts within the psychological tradition toward methods and foci of attention that have been a part of the sociological tradition. With the exception of the expanding area of social cognition, most of the newer areas that psychologists have moved into in recent years are areas where they are increasingly likely to encounter ideas from sociology and other disciplines as well. The rapid expansion of research on relationships in psychology and the rediscovery of the self by psychologists are cases in point. Both topics have historically been a central focus in sociology.

The same can be said for a number of fields of applied social psychology. A cursory examination of books concerned with the psychology of health reveal frequent references to the writings of medical sociologists. Although to a lesser degree, the same kind of exchange seems to be occurring between those in the fields of psychology and the sociology of law. Psychologists are also beginning to develop an interest in the psychology of science; and here, too, they are influenced by developments in the sociology of science, a long-established subdiscipline of sociology.

Finally, the increasing amount of work by psychologists on communication processes reflects a move in the direction of sociolinguistics--an approach favored by sociologically trained social psychologists. While a revival of interest by psychologists in emotions has been around for some time, the recent surge of interest in the sociology of emotions suggests another instance of convergence, this time coming from the sociology side.

Except for a few disciplinary chauvinists, I think we would all agree that this increasing interchange of ideas, concepts, and research findings, and to some extent scientific perspectives, is all to the good. The growth of a science, like that of an organism, is spurred on by hybrid vigor. Students of invention have long known that the rate of growth of new ideas in a society is a function of the size and diversity of its cultural base.

With only a slight reservation, which I note at the close of this chapter, I would argue that we should be seeking ways to expand further the rate of diffusion between the field of psychological social psychology and its sociological counterpart. In considering possible ways of doing this, I shall examine the process and structure of communication that characterizes our science.

It is often useful to think of scientific activity as an endless conversation that goes on in several forums, including the classroom, professional meetings, and the peer review process that is inherent in the funding and publishing of research. The direction of the flow of ideas in this conversational process is greatly influenced by various institutional features, such as the departmental structure of universities, the organization of professional societies, the structure of funding agencies, and the organization of our journals, newsletters, mailing lists, and other manifestations of the so-called invisible colleges that play an increasingly important part in the transmission of ideas. I shall comment on each of these in turn, and suggest how changes in these structures might facilitate communication between the members of these two traditions in social psychology.

First, let's consider the classroom and related instructional settings. It is obvious that if we are going to turn out a new generation of social psychologists with an interdisciplinary base of knowledge, more work in the other discipline should be required of undergraduate majors in psychology and sociology. It has been my experience over the years in reviewing transcripts of students applying to our doctoral program in social psychology that the sociology undergraduate major who has developed an interest in social psychology has had considerable exposure to psychology; whereas, those coming from psychology departments have had very little, if any, work in sociology. The latter is unfortunate if the objective is to turn out a future generation of social psychologists with a broader interdisciplinary orientation. The importance of this feature of undergraduate training should not be underestimated. There is much truth in the old adage concerning how the tree is bent. It has been our experience that despite our efforts to turn out doctoral students with a balanced interdisciplinary orientation, their previous undergraduate training strongly biases them in the direction of one or the other traditions in social psychology.

A complicating factor in addressing this imbalance is a basic fact of institutional demography. There are more students majoring in psychology than in sociology. Even in programs such as ours at the University of Nevada at Reno, where students with an interest in social psychology major in one or the other parent departments but are required to take the same courses in social psychology, all of which are cross listed and taught interchangeably by psychologists and sociologists, the fact that a majority of students come from the Psychology Department gives our training a psychological cast. This, of course, reflects the effects of a basic structural feature of universities, their departmental organization.

There is no question that if we wish to turn the two social psychologies into one, separate departments of social psychology, staffed by both psychologists and sociologists, will be necessary. In a few universities unencumbered by a departmental structure, programs with an interdisciplinary flavor may flourish. Elsewhere the strains on interdisciplinary programs imposed by this structural feature has taken its toll. For a brief period in the history of social psychology, there were several outstanding interdisciplinary programs (those at Michigan and Harvard being examples) which for a period did turn out an interdisciplinary product. But, as we all know, they eventually ended. While I was not privy to the intimate details of their demise, my experience with the strains we have encountered in one of the longest running programs of this sort suggests reasons as to why such programs are generally doomed to eventual failure, except under certain special circumstances.

The most pervasive source of strains stems from the fact that faculty positions and operating and equipment funds are generally lodged in the parent departments. Interdisciplinary programs, unless they are a line item in an institution's budget, must rely on the willingness of the cooperating departments to contribute their share. Almost inevitably non-social psychologists in both departments, anxious to build up their own specialities, tend to resent the diversion of funds to programs outside the department. During periods of fiscal austerity, such as that which most of us in higher education find ourselves in today, this is a particular source of friction; and it is particularly apt to manifest itself when a decision has to be made concerning the filling of new or vacated positions. Only where an interdisciplinary program has departmental status or program independence marked by a separate line item in an institution's budget is the strain from this source likely to be abated. I know during the history of our own program, where this preferable state of affairs has never existed, the periodic crises over the funding of the program have only been resolved either as a result of the chairs of both departments having unusually good working relations, or as a result of having the higher administration intervene on behalf of the interdisciplinary program to force one or the other of the departments to come to its support.

There is one circumstance, fostered in part by the current financial squeeze, under which academic administrators might be supportive of interdisciplinary programs. Where social psychologists from both departments of psychology and sociology are desirous of a graduate program, yet by themselves do not have the critical mass for such a program, they might consider combining forces. It has been my impression that administrators are apt to view an interdisciplinary program as a defensible investment.

A second strain on interdisciplinary programs, given the prevailing departmental organization of institutions of higher education, arises from problems of control, accountability, and evaluation of those participating in such programs. Members of interdisciplinary social psychology programs will inevitably find themselves subject to conflicting demands arising from the program and from their respective departments. This is particularly noticeable when setting up course offerings for each semester. The department may want a social psychologist to teach a course that fills some departmental need, whereas the program requires a course in some area of social psychology. At times like these, another source of strain is apt to be felt. While persons in such programs are dedicated to the development of social psychology, they still have their intellectual roots in either psychology or sociology. These ties and identifications often become apparent when curriculum matters come to the fore, with sociologists tending to feel that the instructional program does not give adequate emphasis to social structural variables, and psychologists perhaps feeling more attention should be devoted to intraindividual processes.

It has also been our experience that there is one problem that has not arisen in connection with an interdisciplinary graduate program. One might expect that the graduates from such programs might have difficulty competing for jobs, since they are neither fish nor fowl. Actually, the reverse seems to be the case. Over the years almost all of the students in our interdisciplinary program have obtained professional positions. There appear to be two reasons for this. First, the methodological skills acquired by our students, particularly the non-laboratory ones favored by sociologists such as skills in survey research, provide our students with an edge in obtaining non-academic jobs in government, industry, and university-based research units. Second, the size of the academic market is increased by virtue of the fact that they can apply for positions in both psychology and sociology departments, and more recently in departments of management and communication. Even with this advantage I am not optimistic about the return of interdisciplinary programs. Thus, this structural change which would have the most effect in increasing the diffusion of theories and findings from one social psychological tradition to the other is, I am afraid, not very likely.

There are, however, other possibilities in the instructional arena. In addition to encouraging students majoring in one department to take more work in the other, there is the possibility of cross-discipline hiring. Permanent or visiting slots can be filled by persons trained in the other discipline. While examples of this are infrequent, they have occurred. Both Jane Piliavin and Elaine Hatfield, trained as psychologists, were hired by the Department of Sociology at the University of Wisconsin. I have been a visiting professor in psychology departments, and there are other such instances. Another perhaps more common, but generally not as effective, way of increasing communication between the two traditions is the use of adjunct, joint, or affiliate appointments wherever possible. Persons from the other discipline involved in such arrangements may offer an occasional course in the department, serve on or chair graduate committees, and give and attend departmental colloquia. A colloquium series in social psychology sponsored jointly by psychology and sociology departments is another mechanism that can be used to increase the contact between psychologists and sociologists on the same campus.

A second arena where psychologically- and sociologically-trained social psychologists are likely to encounter each other is in the funding and publishing of research. This occurs at two levels. First, at the level of peer review, some review committees contain both sociologists and psychologists. Those committees making recommendations for funding by NIMH are good examples. In these review activities, persons from both disciplines are exposed to the views of members of the other. In a more indirect fashion, to the degree that journal editorial boards and lists of reviewers contain representatives from both of the social psychologies, exchanges of information and views are apt to occur. During the review process authors from both disciplines may receive feedback from those in the other discipline. I would judge the amount of influence exchanged in these channels to be fairly minimal. With few exceptions, the editorial boards, and to a lesser extent lists of reviewers, of our various journals tend to be homogeneous in regard to discipline. These exceptions, however, are instructive. Journals that utilize both kinds of social psychologists in the peer review process are either committed on the grounds of scientific ideology to be interdisciplinary, or focus on topical areas that are inherently interdisciplinary. An example of the former would be the *Journal for the Theory of Social Behavior*, and of the latter the *Journal of Social and Personal Relationships*. As more such journals are founded, the volume of exchange across disciplinary lines is likely to increase. As mentioned earlier, I believe this growth in interdisciplinary journals is likely to occur. However, the main line journals in psychology, at least, have retained their editorial homogeneity.

In sociology, the picture is mixed. The editorial board of *Symbolic Interaction* has retained its sociological purity. *Social Psychology Quarterly*, however, has had a sprinkling of psychologists on its editorial board and lists of reviewers. Thus, sociologists publishing in *Social Psychology Quarterly* may encounter in the peer review process some feedback from psychologically-trained social psychologists.

To some extent this feedback may be redundant, since sociologically-trained social psychologists are usually fairly well acquainted with the psychological literature. An admittedly cursory analysis of the citation patterns found in *Social Psychology Quarterly*, compared with the *Journal of Personality and Social Psychology*, suggests that it is a rare article published in the former journal, typically by sociologists, that fails to cite material drawn from the latter. Sociologically-trained social psychologists, at least those likely to publish in *Social Psychology Quarterly*, appear to be familiar with the contents of the *Journal of Personality and Social Psychology*, produced almost exclusively by psychologists. On the other hand, the relatively infrequent citation of articles from *Social Psychology Quarterly* by researchers publishing in the *Journal of Personality and Social Psychology* indicates that this exchange is one sided, with psychologists failing to benefit from relevant works produced by sociologists.

This imbalance in the direction of the influence between psychologists and sociologists is further exacerbated by the fact that articles authored by psychologists are much more apt to appear in *Social Psychology Quarterly* than are articles by sociologists in the *Journal of Personality and Social Psychology*, or the *Journal of Experimental Social Psychology*, or the *Personality and Social Psychology Bulletin*, journals most frequently read by psychologists. If this imbalance is to be remedied, psychologically-trained social psychologists must be encouraged to pay more attention to what is being published in *Social Psychology Quarterly* and *Symbolic Interaction* as well. Sociologists, in turn, should submit more of their work to the major social psychology journals in psychology.

A third forum where psychologically- and sociologically-trained social psychologists are apt to encounter each other consists of the activities of professional groups. These activities range from the annual meetings of the national and regional associations of the parent disciplines, through meetings and other activities of organizations devoted to social psychology in general, down to smaller organizations concerned with a particular sub-area of research. It has been my impression that relatively few sociologists are members of APA. Though the number of psychologists who belong to ASA is larger, the annual meetings of these two organizations, as is the case with their regional counterparts, are not forums for much intellectual exchange. Given the increase over the years in the membership dues of both APA and ASA and the limited availability of travel funds, I am not optimistic that this picture will change. At the same time, it might be possible to increase the amount of dialogue between the two social psychologies if the leadership and program organizers of Division Eight of APA and the social psychology section of ASA were to sponsor sessions that brought the perspectives of both disciplines to bear on selected topics. With the exception of the Society for the Study of Symbolic Interaction, those professional groups composed exclusively of social psychologists have, from the outset, been committed to the idea of including both psychologists and sociologists. This was certainly the case for the Society of Experimental Social Psychology. However, over the years the proportion of sociologically oriented members has steadily declined, largely as a result of the almost exponential growth in the number of psychologists being admitted. Today, with a membership approaching five hundred, there are about 20 or so sociologists, and only a handful of these attend the annual meetings of SESP with any regularity. It appears from the pages of the newsletter of the Society for the Advancement of Social Psychology that sociologists have been more active in that organization; but even here the dominant orientation by far is the psychological perspective. This state of affairs is almost inevitable, given the relative size and rate of growth in these two sectors of social psychology. Based on the relative size of the division of personality and social psychology of APA, and the social psychology section of ASA, the ratio of psychologically-trained social psychologists to their sociological counterparts is about eight to one. This ratio is undoubtedly inflated because the total membership in Division Eight includes those whose primary interest is personality rather than social psychology and the ASA Section does not include all symbolic interactionists. Yet even if the true ratio were four to one, sociologically-trained social psychologists would still constitute a small minority. Given this fact, it behooves organizations committed to the development of social psychology to insure that both social psychologies are adequately represented, and to bend over backwards in combatting the effects of this demographic fact of our science.

When we come to those organizations committed to the development of a particular sub-area of social psychology, we encounter, at least in some of these areas, a considerably greater interdisciplinary mix and the maximum opportunity for mutually advantageous exchanges between psychologists and sociologists. Of those with whom I have had personal experience, one of the oldest is the West Coast Conference for Small Group Research, which has been meeting alternately for the past twenty-five years with either the Pacific Sociological Association, or the Western Psychological Association. Of more recent vintage is the newly formed International Society of Social and Personal Relationships and SIG, an acronym for Self Interest Group. At present, the latter group is simply a mailing list to facilitate the exchange of papers between researchers, both here and abroad, who are interested in the self. While the last two groups are composed largely of psychologically-trained social psychologists, the number of sociologists included is roughly commensurate with the overall existing ratio of sociologists to psychologists in the disciplines of social psychology.

Let me close with one further comment concerning the implications of this current disciplinary ratio. It can be expected that without special efforts, the contributions coming from the sociological side of the fence to the overall development of social psychology may be greatly diminished. Yet at the same time, given the minority status of sociological social psychology, if we are ever successful in overcoming the barrier between the carriers of these two traditions, it might be at the cost of losing some of the key elements of the distinctive perspective which characterizes sociological social psychology. Given the earlier discussion in this chapter concerning some of the barriers, I am not unduly concerned about this. Rather, I am somewhat encouraged by the prospect of an increase, though modest in amount, in the flow of minority influences from sociology to psychology without catastrophic acculturation and ultimate assimilation.

References

Backman, C.W. (1983). Toward an interdisciplinary social psychology. In L. Berkowitz (Ed.), *Advances in experimental social psychology* (Vol. 16) (pp. 220-261). New York: Academic Press.

Lindzey, G. & Aronson, E. (Eds.). (1985). *The handbook of social psychology* (3rd ed.). New York: Random House.

Michener, T. A., DeLamater, M. D., & Schwartz. (1986). *Psychology*. New York: Harcourt Brace and Jovanovich.

Stephan, C. W. & Stephan, W. G. (1985). *Two social psychologies*. Homewood, IL: Dorsey Press.

Stryker, S. (1983). Social psychology from the standpoint of a structural symbolic interaction: Toward an interdisciplinary social psychology. In L. Berkowitz (Ed.), *Advances in experimental social psychology* (Vol. 16) (pp. 181-218). New York: Academic Press.

6
Interdisciplinary Lessons: The Two Social Psychologies from the Perspective of a Psychologist Practicing Sociology

Carmi Schooler

Although my graduate training was to a large extent in psychological social psychology and my graduate degree itself from a department of psychology, through a combination of accident and intellectual proclivity a substantial portion of my professional career has taken place in the arena of sociology. Over forty percent of the papers in my bibliography are in sociological publications. This split in my professional identity has given me an unusual vantage point from which to observe the relationships between the two fields and their respective sub-disciplines of social psychology.

My experience has lead me to the conclusion that a major contributing factor to the difficulties between the two social psychologies is the very fact that they are embedded in different overall disciplines. Each of these disciplines has its own history, perspective and way of doing things. Members of each discipline are likely to know more about other sub-fields in their own discipline than about what is taking place in the *other* social-psychology. Such allegiances and the absence of interdisciplinary perspective affect the nature of social psychologists' own research as well as their views of the *other* social psychology. Seen from this vantage point, differences between the general fields of sociology and psychology are critically relevant to the question of the gap between the two social psychologies.

If we are concerned about closing the gap between the two social psychologies, we should probably accept that differences between the disciplines of sociology and psychology rooted in such *guild issues* as competition for resources or jobs are not readily amenable to amelioration. Difficulties due to structural differences such as size or proportion of practitioners are also likely to remain with us. However, much that is problematic in the relationship of the two social psychologies is due to differences in the intellectual traditions of the disciplines of which each is a part. Such difficulties between the two social psychologies could be at least partially ameliorated if social psychologists would pay some attention not only to what they could learn from social psychologists in the other discipline, but also to what they could learn from the broader discipline in which their fellow social psychologists are enmeshed.

The intellectual gap between the two disciplines affected my own social-psychological research, influencing even such relatively mundane decisions as where to submit a paper for possible publication. Thus, although I was well aware that much of the research I was involved with in the 1970's on the psychological effects of occupational conditions was of direct relevance to psychological social psychology, as well as to industrial and organizational psychology, I refrained from sending these papers to psychological journals. This decision was in large measure due to my reluctance to get embroiled in the methodological discussions that I believed would be necessary to convince psychologists about the greater level of statistical sophistication that marked the data analytic techniques then being used in sociology. The irony of this methodological gap between these two disciplines hurt the psychologist within me. When in the late 1950's, I first became familiar with the quantitative methods then used in sociology, it seemed perfectly clear to me that any reasonably trained psychologist who had probably been exposed, not only to a variety of non-parametric techniques, but also to analysis of variance, correlation, multiple regression, and possibly even factor analysis, could run rings methodologically around most sociologists. It was, indeed, my familiarity with these techniques that served as the basis of my confidence in the plausibility of empirically testing Kohn's (1963) interpretation about the nature of the social structural determinants of parental values. My professional involvement in sociology is due, in large part, to my involvement with him in empirically testing and expanding to other areas of psychological functioning the social-psychological hypothesis that differences in occupational experiences underlie many of the relationships found between social stratification and psychological functioning (Kohn & Schooler, 1983).

I was of course naive about the explanatory potential for the causal analysis of non-experimental data of the statistics then being used by psychologists. The intervening years have seen a complete reversal in the relative levels of methodological sophistication of the two fields as sociologists came to grips with such interrelated problems as causal modeling, measurement error, latent class analysis of qualitative data, and event history analysis. It took this near revolution in sociological methodology to make it possible for Kohn and me to deal with the substantive problem we had set ourselves. Although there are now some signs of change in psychology, the level of quantitative sophistication visible in the sociological literature seems almost qualitatively different from that visible in the psychological. In this area, sociologists have very little to learn from psychology.

The same is true for the related issue of sampling. Sociology, with its history of survey based research, has a long and continuing concern with this problem. However, for most psychological researchers, who tend to be experimentalists, sampling seems to be a non-issue--a matter of almost no concern. The samples of convenience psychologists frequently use, and the generalizations they seem to be willing to make from such samples, constitute substantial problems.

Closely connected to the methodological problem of sampling is the central substantive lesson that psychology should learn from sociology--concern about the larger social contexts that psychologists should, but rarely do, take into account, in building theories, planning research and explaining findings. This is even true for psychological social psychologists, who one might expect would be more aware of the possibility of such social effects than would other members of their discipline. In an excellent review, Sears (1987) has shown that since the early 1960's, the great majority of social psychological studies have relied exclusively on college students tested in the laboratory and that the most prestigious research is, if anything, more likely to have done so. He also presents a variety of evidence suggesting the possibility that such "subjects are likely to have less crystallized attitudes, less formulated senses of self, stronger cognitive skills, stronger tendencies to comply with authority, and more unstable peer group relationships than do older adults..." He concludes that "(t)hese peculiarities of social psychology's predominant database may have unwittingly, and perhaps misleadingly, contributed to such major substantive conclusions as that people are easily influenced, behave inconsistently with their attitudes, do not rest their self-perceptions on introspection, and are highly egocentric. This database may also contribute to the strong emphasis in contemporary social psychology upon cognitive processes..." A more general discussion of the mutual relevance of social structural effects and experimental situations can be found in Schooler (1988).

One issue standing in the way of psychology taking the important lessons of sociology seriously is the approach taken by some sociologists to psychopathology. The problem, of course, does not lie in the honorable history of sociologically based epidemiological studies from Faris and Dunham (1939), through Kohn (1973) to Robins (1985) and Eaton (1985). Nor does it come from psychologists' reactions to Rosenberg's (1984) elegant symbolic interactionist view of psychosis, nor to Kessler's (1982) sociologically oriented, methodologically sophisticated studies of distress and depression. Although they may not be perfect, these studies provide much from which the fields of psychology and of psychiatry can learn. Labeling theory, however, is another matter. Its strongly stated original formulation (Scheff, 1966, 1984) that mental illness occurs because those that society labels as mentally ill are constrained to adopt that role is a stumbling block to those working directly with the suffering of the mentally ill taking the discipline of sociology seriously. Modified labeling theory (Link, Cullen, Streuning, Shrout & Dohrenwend, 1989) which examines the interaction of social stigmatization on the functioning and health seeking behavior of those already ill is yet another matter--one worth investigating.

Turning to what the discipline of sociology can learn from the discipline of psychology, besides sociological social psychology, the fields of psychology from which I think sociologists can learn the most are personality and abnormal psychology, cognitive psychology, and comparative psychology--not of cultures but of animal species. What can be learned from all but the latter is most directly germane to those sociologists who are social psychologists, in the sense that they are concerned with how the social system effects the individual's psychological functioning, and I will return to these lessons later. Surprisingly, it is the lessons that can be learned from comparative psychology that have the most widespread application to sociology, being relevant not only to sociological social psychology, but to sociology as a whole.

Comparative psychology which is presently embattled, both conceptually and in terms of academic opportunities, with ethology, sociobiology and behavioral biology, is useful in three ways. The first use, a substantive one, is as an antidote to the exaggerated claims of sociobiology. The second use, a research focusing one, is the insistence that the mechanisms that determine social and individual behavior be explicitly spelled out rather than leaving explanations in such reified terms as imprinting, instinct or social influence. The third use is providing a sophisticated substantive and analytic view of the qualitatively different levels of complexity at which phenomena are organized.

Interestingly, all of these lessons come from the work of one man, T.

Christian Schneirla, who, through a combination of dumb luck and incurable dilettantism, I was fortunate to have as a teacher in graduate school. I am, however, not the first to call some of Schneirla's views (1972) to the attention of sociology. Featherman and Lerner (1985) have already made good use of Schneirla's conclusion that individual development is inherently a social process at all levels of manifestation, including the biological, in their paper on ontogenesis and sociogenesis. I, however, would like to extend the discussion of Schneirla's thoughts on the importance of both specifically spelling out mechanisms (1965) and taking into account level of organization for understanding behavior (Tobach & Schneirla, 1968; see also Tobach & Greenberg, 1984; Tobach, 1982) and to use his ideas as a staging point for the rest of my paper.

Central to Schneirla's own empirical research was his examination and explanation of the foraging behavior of army ants--"the most complex instance of organized mass behavior occurring regularly outside the homesite in any insect, or for that matter any infra-human animal" (Schneirla, 1940). He was able to clearly elucidate how the complex patterns of behavior that such colonies show, both in terms of the division of labor within the colony and in the way colonies interact with their physical and biological environments, are determined rather directly by anatomical and physiological factors affecting the individual's tendency to approach or withdraw from different stimuli, and not by such amorphous determinants as *instinct* or *superorganism*. On the basis of his own further research, as well as of his encyclopedic knowledge of the field, Schneirla was able to fit these findings into a more general theory linking levels of neuronal and social organization. According to this theory (Schneirla, 1965; Tobach & Schneirla, 1968), among the simplest animals the form of social "organization" is passive aggregation, where external physical phenomena, winds or tides for example, move individual organisms next to each other. The next level of social organization is active aggregation, where animals assume a spatial relationship to each other as a result of responses of individual organisms to stimulation from an inanimate external source. This is the simplest form of what Schneirla calls taxis-directed orientation reactions involving movement of the organism. The next level of organization of animal aggregates is the bio-social, which comes about as a result of biotaxis, where the source of stimulation is animate, for example chemical secretions. At this biosocial level the pattern of action of the aggregates is typically determined rather directly by structural and physiologic actors. It is at this level that the ant colonies operate. The next level of social organization is psychotaxic. At this level reactions to taxic and biotaxic stimuli are modified through the integration of maturation and experience by virtue of higher level psychological processes such as conditioning, learning and concept formation, processes that introduce a plasticity of behavior not visible in simpler forms of organization. At a still higher level of social organization communicable meanings rather than the immediate physiological effect of stimuli come to determine behavior.

If we compare ants and humans, we find not merely quantitative, but qualitative differences in the levels of functioning of both the individual and the social system. Among ants the behavior of individuals and of whole colonies is stereotyped and essentially changeless unless new developments occur through genetic evolution. Even where workers are capable of learning fairly complex individually different routes, the results cannot be communicated to others. Consequently new advances by the individual in learning a route contribute substantially nothing to the colony except individual increments of food, and the special learning of each individual dies with it. On the other hand, although humans have been unchanged genetically for millennia, the functioning of their social systems change as a result of the experiences of individual members. Furthermore, the ways in which human social systems amass, integrate and use information supplied by individuals are constantly evolving (for example the development of writing, long distance communication, computers), leading to ever more complex levels of organization.

The concept of "levels" is important to Schneirla. He uses it for differentiating both the levels of neuronal complexity of the participant organisms and the levels of organization of the social systems in which the participants interact. In attaching such importance to the concept, Schneirla reopened general questions about the meaning of levels of organization and integration which had been raised over the years by a variety of scientists (Needham, 1937; Novikoff, 1945; Simon, 1973). In his review of how Schneirla and others have used the concept, Aronson (1984) summarizes the concept of levels of organization as follows:

1. Except for trivialities, all material entities and all processes in the universe may be arranged hierarchically with respect to levels of integration, differentiation and organizational complexity.

2. The levels, which are a function of time, and which form by the accumulation of differences during the course of evolution, transform into new and complex products qualitatively different from their predecessors. Much evidence indicates that these transformations occur

suddenly when the accumulation of quantitative differences reach a critical phase (N.B. see Prigogine & Stagers, 1984, for a recent and comprehensive mathematical and philosophical discussion of how such transformations occur.)

3. Higher levels of organization are more than simple quantitative accretions. Rather they represent qualitative changes in the complexity of integration... so that the new level has its own unique properties, laws, and principles, which can not be predicted from even the most complete knowledge of the lower levels that preceded it (Aronson, 1984:67).

Accepting this viewpoint has a variety of implications for both sociologists and psychologists. One such is that the level at which research is carried out should be a function of the question being asked. Thus, if one is interested in understanding neuronal action, it may be appropriate to start with the conveniently large neuron of some species of jelly fish. However, if one wants to understand how an organized set of neurons operates, using a jelly fish as a model for the more complexly organized ant or human brains won't do. Furthermore, studying the functioning of a neuron in the brain is not the same as studying the functioning of the brain. On the other hand, since the characteristics of the brain neuron affect how the brain operates, how the brain operates is in part a function of the characteristics of its component neurons. At the same time, if one is interested in how the brain works one has to take into account its relationship to the larger systems of which it is a part, for example, the body or the social system.

In a similar manner, the social system of humans is in part a function of their biochemical, neurological and psychological levels. Hence its mode of operation, being affected by the nature of these component systems, is different from that of the ant bio-social system. Furthermore, just as the characteristics of the components may affect the characteristics of the larger system, the characteristics of the larger system may affect the characteristics of the components. Thus, Humphrey (1976) has suggested that a primary reason for the growth of intelligence in primates may have been that the complexity of the social systems they evolved provided a selective reproductive advantage to those animals who were smart enough to effectively manage the resultant social intricacies. [1]

According to this comparative psychology based theory of levels, it is completely legitimate for sociologists to study the behavior of a social system at a level of inquiry that ignores both the psychological characteristics of the individual participants and the social and cultural characteristics of the larger social systems in which the social system under study is embedded. While doing so, however, they should bear in mind that the characteristics of both more and less complex levels of phenomena affect the operation of intermediate ones.

It is just such interlevel effects that I find intriguing. On the one hand, I am curious about the causal connections between particular socioeconomic systems, such as Japan's, and the more complex sociocultural systems of which they are a part (Schooler, in press). On the other hand, I am interested in the nature of the reciprocal causal connections between a particular social system (the socioeconomic system) and the psychological functioning of the individuals who are parts of it (Schooler & Naoi, 1988).

It is in this latter concern for examining the causal connections between social structure and individual psychological functioning that the other lessons of Schneirla's approach must be taken into consideration. We should not be satisfied with explanations based on reification and the coining of terms that evade the question of what happened and how.

This is also where the lessons from the other fields of psychology are relevant for sociological social psychologists. Clearly, knowing something about what is going on in psychological social psychology is important, but it is not enough. If, following Marx (1964), Mannheim (1954) and Merton (1968), sociologists are concerned with how individuals' vantage points in the social system affect their belief systems, then they must understand the psychological laws through which people generalize what they have learned in one context to another. This is one of the central issues in cognitive psychology (see Schooler 1988). Personality and abnormal psychology have also each gathered a substantial body of knowledge and developed some interesting models of individual psychological functioning. Although sociologists have also made important substantive and theoretical contributions in several of these areas, it is imperative that sociologists concerned with normal and abnormal psychological functioning be aware of what is taking place in sister disciplines. I realize that, given the constraints of time and energy that we all face, such advice is easier to give than to follow. Still, there is probably a limit to how rewarding it can be, both personally and professionally, to discover that one has reinvented the wheel.

Finally, something may be learned from research that combines the questions and techniques of the two social psychologies and their respective disciplines--psychology and sociology. For instance, although

Kohn, I, and our associates (1983), have demonstrated that occupational self-direction leads to intellectual flexibility and a self-directed orientation to self and society, we have not elucidated the exact mechanisms through which this takes place, nor how these changes affect the individual's interrelationships with others. Doing so would involve a challenging combination of both social psychologies and of cognitive psychology as well. It would also require that close attention be paid to the concerns that Schneirla showed to be so important for comparative psychology--the concern for describing mechanisms at the proper level of specificity and the concern for understanding the differences in organizing principles that exist among different levels of phenomena.

Notes

[1] Although what takes place at a given level cannot be deduced merely from knowledge of the lower levels, prediction may be possible if knowledge of higher levels is also used. Since what takes place at more complex levels of organization affects what takes place at lower ones, it is not clear whether the rules governing a particular level of phenomena are directly deducible from knowledge of the rules of both the higher and the lower levels of organization.

References

Aronson, L. R. (1984). Levels of integration and organization: A reevaluation of the evolutionary scale. In G. Greenberg & E. Tobach (Eds.), *Behavioral evolution and integrativelevels* (pp. 57-81). Hillsdale, NJ: Erlbaum.

Eaton, W. W. (1985). *The sociology of mental disorders*. New York: Praeger.

Faris, R. E. L. & Dunham, H. W. (1939). *Mental disorders in urban area: An ecological study of schizophrenia and other psychoses*. Chicago: University of Chicago Press.

Featherman, D. and Lerner, R. M. (1985). Ontogenesis and sociogenesis: Problematics for theory and research about development and socialization across the lifespan. *American Sociological Review*, *50*, 659-676.

Humphrey, N. K. (1976). The social function of intellect. In P. P. G. Bateson & P. K. Klopfer (Eds.), *Growing points in ethology* (pp. 303-321). Cambridge: Cambridge University Press.

Kessler, R. C. (1982). A disaggregation of the relationship between socioeconomic status and psychological distress. *American Sociological Review*, *47*, 752-764.

Kohn, Melvin L. (1963). Social class and parent-child relationships: An interpretation. *American Journal of Sociology*, *68*, 471-480.

Kohn, Melvin L. (1973). Social class and schizophrenia: A critical review and a reformulation. *Schizophrenia Bulletin*, *7*, 60-79.
Kohn, M. L. & Schooler, C. (1983). In collaboration with J. Miller, K. A. Miller, C. Schoenbach, & R. Schoenberg. *Work and personality: An inquiry into the impact of social stratification*. Norwood, NJ: Ablex.
Link, B. G., Cullen, F. T., Streuning, E., Shrout, P. E., & Dohrenwend, B. P. (1989). A modified labeling theory approach to mental disorders: An empirical assessment. *American Sociological Review*, *54*, 400-423.
Mannheim, K. (1954). *Ideology and utopia: An introduction to the sociology of knowledge*. New York: Harcourt.
Marx, K. (1964). *Early writings*. Edited and translated by T. B. Bottomore. New York: McGraw Hill.
Merton, R. (1968). *Social theory and social structure*. New York: Free Press.
Needham, J. (1937). *Integrative levels: A revaluation of the idea of progress*. Oxford: Clarendon Press.
Novikoff, A. B. (1945). The concept of integrative levels and biology. *Science*, *101*, 209-215.
Prigogine, I. and Stagers, I. (1984). *Order out of chaos*. New York: Bantam Books.
Robins, L. N. (1985, April). *The DIS in epidemiological studies*. Paper presented at the International Symposium on Psychiatric Epidemiology, Taipei, Taiwan.
Rosenberg, M. (1984). A symbolic interactionist view of psychosis. *Journal of Health and Social Behavior*, *25*, 289-302.
Scheff, T. (1966). *Being mentally ill: A sociological theory*. Chicago: Aldine.
Scheff, T. (1984). *Being mentally ill: A sociological theory* (2nd ed.). Chicago: Aldine.
Schneirla, T. C. (1940). Further studies on the army-ant behavior pattern. *Journal of Comparative Psychology*, *29*, 401-460.
Schneirla, T. C. (1951). The *levels* concept in the study of social organization in animals. In M. Sherif & J. N. Rohrer (Eds.), *Social psychology at the crossroads*. New York: Harper.
Schneirla, T. C. (1965). Aspects of stimulation and organization in approach/withdrawal processes underlying vertebrate behavioral development. In D. S. Lehrman, R. Hinde & E. Shaw (Eds.), *Advances in the study of behavior* (pp. 1-71). New York: Academic Press.
Schneirla, T. C. (1972). *Selected writings*. L. R. Aronson, E. Tobach, D. S., Lehrman & J. S. Rosenblatt (Eds.). San Francisco: Freeman Press.
Schooler, C. (1989). Social structural effects and experimental situations: Mutual lessons of cognitive and social science. In K. W. Schaie & C. Schooler (Eds.), *Structure and aging: Psychological processes*. Hillsdale, NJ: Erlbaum.
Schooler, C. (in press). The individual in Japanese history; parallels to and divergences from the European experience. *Sociological Forum*.
Schooler, C. & Naoi, A. (1988). The psychological effects of traditional and economically peripheral job settings in Japan. *American Journal of Sociology*, *94*, 335-355.

Sears, D. O. (1987). Implications of the life-span approach for research on attitudes of social cognition. In R. P. Abeles (Ed.), *Life-span perspectives and social psychology*. Hillsdale, NJ: Erlbaum.

Simon, H. A. (1973). The organization of complex systems. In H. Pattee (Ed.), *Hierarchy theory: The challenge of complex systems*. New York: George Braziller.

Tobach, E. (1982). The synthetic theory in evolution and psychology as a science. In H. Schmidt G. Tembrock (Ed.), *Evolution and determination of animal and human behaviour*. New York: Elsevier.

Tobach, E. & Schneirla, T. C. (1968) The biopsychology of social behavior of animals. in R. E. Cooke & S. Levin (Eds.), *Biological basis of pediatric practice*.

Tobach, E. & Greenberg, G. (1984). The significance of T. C. Schneirla's contribution to the concept of levels of integration. In G. Greenberg & E. Tobach (Eds.), *Behavioral evolution and integrativelevels* (pp. 1-7). Hillsdale, NJ: Erlbaum.

7
Consequences of the Gap Between The "Two Social Psychologies"

Sheldon Stryker

My message is simple: that there are two social psychologies ain't necessarily bad.

Inherent in that message are a number of sub-messages, either explicit or implicit, which it will be the burden of this paper to explicate:

1. There are indeed two social psychologies, and while the two are not totally unlike, important differences exist between them.
2. A negative evaluation is generally placed on this state of affairs: i. e., the consequences of the existence of the two different social psychologies are thought to be detrimental for the separate social psychologies as well as for an ideal single discipline of social psychology.
3. This typical evaluation overlooks, or disregards, the very real possibility that along with whatever negative consequences accrue as a result of the gap between the two social psychologies, that gap has a number of important positive consequences. These positive consequences hold for the ideal single social psychology as well as for the separate social psychologies.

Not explicit in the message with which I started but implied by the analysis of the last sub-message is a fourth assertion, which will exist in this paper more as inference than as object of thorough discussion:

4. The claimed positive consequences require a sustained "creative" tension between institutional mechanisms linking the two social psychologies and institutional mechanisms keeping them apart.

Taking each of these sub-messages in its turn: A notable aspect of the social psychological landscape over the last ten to twelve years has been the thesis of the two social psychologies. Descriptively, this involves the perception of a series of disjunctures between the social psychology emanating from an institutional base in psychology and the social psychology that is supported by an institutional base in sociology. The thesis was never intended, at least in its more subtle formulation, as a literal assertion that there existed two internally undifferentiated, maximally differentiated bodies of intellectual traditions and styles of thinking about and doing social psychology that are isomorphic with disciplinary identifications. It did, however, assert a separation in dominant tendencies between (on the one hand) a psychological social psychology defined by its focus on individual psychological processes, with its central task taken to be the comprehension of the impact of social stimuli on those individual psychological processes and its central mode of attaining that comprehension the laboratory experiment, and (on the other hand) a sociological social psychology defined by the reciprocity of society and individual, its fundamental task being the explanation of social interaction, and its methodological reliance on naturalistic observation and survey methods.

Evaluatively, as already suggested, the theme of the two social psychologies involved (and continues to involve) the pronouncement that each of the separate social psychologies suffers from its ignorance of and its isolation from the other, and that an ideal social psychology cannot develop in the absence of an intellectual, and perhaps even an institutional, integration of the two.

Interestingly, and assuming that this coverage and informal content analysis of the relevant literature are accurate, the emphasis has been on the impoverishment of a psychological social psychology deprived of intellectual nourishment from its sociological counterpart, less so on the costs to sociological social psychology that accrue as a consequence of its separation from psychological influences. There are, I think, good reasons for this emphasis. One is surely the focus, sometimes Marxist although not inevitably so, on the collectivity running through the general intellectual scene of the past twenty years. Another reason is the sense of disillusionment within psychological social psychology with the progress of a "truly" scientific social psychology so much a part of the so-called crisis in social psychology that existed in the 1970's. This crisis itself incorporated a sense of the disutilities attending the predominant reliance on experimental procedures, as well as a sense of the need to contextualize social psychological knowledge. Yet another reason, not unrelated to the last, is the cognitive revolution in psychology; originating outside of psychological social psychology (again a point of some import to the argument being made, as will be noted later), it opened the realization in that subdiscipline that whatever the language in which such ideas were couched or the success in treating those ideas with the precision they deserved, sociological social psychology had long given central position to cognitive processes underlying human social behavior.

Whatever its source, the emphasis on the sustenance available to psychological social psychology from the sociological side of the more general field, rather than the reverse, is well taken. This judgment does not depend on an intellectual--i.e., content based--justification. For better or for worse, sociological practitioners of social psychology over the years have tended to be more aware of and more influenced by the theory and the research developed by their psychological brethren than the other way around; this holds for the progression from Watson through Freud through the Allports through Sherif and Newcomb through Heider through Kelley and Thibaut and Jones through Zajonc through Gergen. This, too, is a point to which I will return, for it is a source, though certainly not the only source, of the argument and conclusion that there are significant utilities attached to the continuation of two separate, however inseparable, social psychologies, utilities that would be seriously threatened if the implicit plea for a unified social psychology that is part of the two social psychologies theme were satisfied.

Neither the descriptive nor the evaluative aspect of the theme of the two social psychologies is uniquely a product of the recent past, although almost certainly pronouncements of the current theme have fallen on many more sympathetic ears during the last ten years than did earlier versions of the theme, likely as a consequence of the collectivist intellectual current, the eschatology of the crisis in social psychology plaint, and the shift in psychological social psychology from a behaviorist to a cognitive metaphysics and epistemology that legitimated conceptions like mind and symbol.

One of the more significant precursors of the dual emphases contained in the two social psychologies theme was the post-World War II call for an interdisciplinary social psychology, an intellectual and organizational enterprise that would in fact carry out the promise of virtually every introductory text's definition and at least some texts' coverage of the field. This call was sounded in the writings of Sherif and of Newcomb, to name only two among many. (It is of more than casual interest that the psychologists in the forefront of the interdisciplinary movement of the time were persons who did most of their work outside of the laboratory context.) The call received institutional incarnation in the setting up of formal programs and faculty, even sometimes departments, that joined psychologists and sociologists and occasionally included anthropologists or representatives of other disciplines. The formal programs at Harvard, Michigan and Cornell illustrate the trend, and perhaps provided the impetus for the less dramatic setting up of interdisciplinary "committees" or collaborative research groups at, for example, institutions like Minnesota. This reminder of an earlier version of the two social psychologies theme is introduced to draw later on lessons it may contain relevant to one or another of my own messages; William Sewell, a participant in that early interdisciplinary movement, has recently provided an account of it along with an analysis of why it could not be sustained (Sewell, 1989).

An even more immediate although somewhat more indirect precursor of the current two social psychologies theme was the emergence in Europe of a distinctive social psychological voice. That distinctive voice, sounded in the writings of Moscovici, Tajfel, Israel and others (see, for example, the essays in Israel and Tajfel, 1972), called for the recognition of the significance of the larger social settings, the culture and the organized social structures of societies within which people acted, as determinants of social psychological processes, and therefore constituted a call for the incorporation of sizable sociological components into what was deemed an over-individualistic intellectual enterprise. There is perhaps a touch of irony in all of this, assuming that my sense of history is correct: If I understand things properly, this "distinctive" European social psychology with its emphasis on matters sociological has underwritten in part the recent belief among American trained psychological social psychologists that they "need" sociology. But this distinctive European social psychology grew out of a belief among European scholars that as social psychology in Europe recovered from the destruction of the pre-World War II period and from the war itself, it bore the stamp of a highly individualistic, laboratory-based American version of social psychology; and it grew out of the frustration of these scholars with the dominance of this version of social psychology and their search for an independent voice.

Whatever the relationship between the earlier call for an interdisciplinary social psychology and the more recent two social psychologies arguments, there has long been and continues to be an awareness that, in general, psychologists and sociologists go about the business of social psychology in quite different ways, and that there is only minimal and superficial contact between the distinctive bodies of work (and the sets of persons who produce these bodies of work).

It bears repeating that the image of separation that has been developed can be overdrawn. It also bears repeating that there is very considerable validity to that image. Neither of these iterations will be defended, for want of inclination as much as for the want of time. What Louis Armstrong is reputed to have said about those who asked the question, "What is jazz?," is applicable here. Armstrong's perhaps apocryphal response to that question was, "If they have to ask, they'll never know!" I will, however, illustrate the depth of the separation with two brief anecdotes, neither apocryphal, each coming out of personal experience in interdisciplinary contact. Both anecdotes speak to the underlying truth in Armstrong's response as applied in the case under discussion. They speak as well, not only to the existence of the gap between the two social psychologies, but to some of the essential sources of the gap as well as to the problems in trying to bridge that gap.

Both stories have the same structure: they both involve extensive conversations between myself and psychologists, in which communication seemed to have taken place through the use of common language; and they both involve the slowly emerging realization that despite appearances no real communication had occurred.

One protracted conversation over a number of months involved an attempt to prepare a statement envisioning prospects for the development of social psychology through the next period of years. I, "representing" sociological social psychology, sought to infuse the statement with a reasonable measure of the sociologist's version of social psychology; and I did so by arguing the import of interactionist theory. Interactionist theory, I presumed, had a well-defined, commonly understood content; and I was right. The problem was that its well-defined, commonly understood content was different for me and for my psychological counterpart. Thus, I would repeatedly make my argument, would get what I took to be assent to that argument, only to find in successive drafts of a document being prepared little that reflected interactionist theory; and I could not understand why. My understanding has come only after the fact. I intended "interactionist theory" as a shorthand description of the central ideas of Cooley and Mead, the ideas that social interaction is the essential nexus between "society" and "person," indeed that both society and person are emergents from that interaction, that human social behavior is an important degree to be understood as a product of utilizing in the context of interaction resources ("real" and symbolic) made available and circumscribed by society and by prior interactions, and that the processes of interaction themselves could both reproduce and alter prior (that is, existing before the interaction itself) patterns of interaction and interaction outcomes. For my psychological counterpart, interaction theory referred to the argument that personality characteristics interacted with characteristics of the situation to produce outcomes of social psychological interest--that such outcomes were the resultant of a calculus joining the main effects of individual personality and of situation and an interaction term representing their joint product, and, indeed, that little of consequence exists beyond the main effects themselves. Thus, my present understanding of our protracted conversation is that the two of us, the psychologist and I, consistently and continuously talked past one another, and did so in the worst possible way: both of us assumed that because we used common terms, we shared a system of meanings of those terms; we failed to communicate substantively despite talking to one another.

The second anecdote involves the basic sociological conception of "social structure." Defined variously by sociologists, the conception has a core referent in relatively stable, recurrent, patterned social relationships that demarcate sets of persons (or "parts" of persons in the form of positions and rules) within a society. The generalized phenomena *and* the generalized significance of the reality to which the concept of social structure refers is that social interaction is specialized, that the probabilities are that only certain kinds of persons will find themselves in only certain kinds of social locations or situations with only certain kinds of material and symbolic interactional resources (e.g., money, authority, skills, values, selves, symbols, whatever), and that therefore probable outcomes of their interaction with others are heavily circumscribed. Thus, the language of age structure, power structure, class structure, ecological structure--all these terms and more--argue the existence within society of constraints/facilitators with respect to social interaction and its products, including the kinds of "personalities" people come to have or even have real possibilities of coming to have. Clearly, the very conception of social structure argues that there is a social reality going beyond individual psychological processes that importantly conditions the latter; and recognition of this argument implies the absolute necessity of going beyond individual psychological processes for the understanding of those processes themselves, not to speak of understanding processes of social interaction.

The second anecdote can now be completed quickly. I have been involved in literally hundreds of conversations over past years--in the context of grant committee discussions, or as a site visitor in connection with grant applications, or as a member of dissertation committees, or in classrooms, or simply as part of over-a-drink-banter--in which communication broke down and could not seem to be repaired when the psychologists involved "heard" or immediately translated the conception of social structure into the very different conception of *perception* of social structure. Perhaps as a consequence of their implicit acceptance of the Lewinian doctrine that the only psychological reality is that which enters the psychological fields of individuals, the social (read, sociological) reality of social structure was dissolved into the universal solvent of perception. (Within sociology, some symbolic interactionists accomplish the same dissolving of social structure through the conception of definition of the situation.) I do not believe it problematic to assert--nor is it difficult to evidence the assertion--that, however important and consequential the perceptions of social class, social class exists and importantly impacts social psychological processes and outcomes independently from perceptions of social class. Yet, it is extraordinarily difficult to make that point in a way that gets reflected in the thinking of social psychologists trained in psychology.

The stories are not intended as complaints or indictments. It is absolutely certain that their equivalents, reversing the positions of the protagonists, and likely focusing on the obtuseness of sociologists in the face of individual differences, can be provided by psychologist-readers. They are intended to speak to the reality of the gap between the two social psychologies, to the considerable problems involved in efforts to bridge the gap, and--at least implicitly--to some of the sources of that gap.

In particular, these stories point to the different intellectual traditions of a sociological social psychology and a psychological social psychology, at the same time pointing to the differing intellectual traditions of their parent disciplines, as a major source of the gap. As a sociologist, impressed by the importance of social structure in circumscribing interaction, I would stress as underlying this difference the institutional barriers to interaction and communication that were part of my earlier analysis (Stryker, 1977) of the two social psychologies. These include the existence of each of the social psychologies in separate academic departments (that are themselves as likely as not to be part of separate academic divisions), the existence of separate publication outlets. It seems clear to me that the undeniably important intergroup cognitions stressed by Stephan and Stephan (in this volume) are themselves strongly influenced by these institutional barriers and indeed could not be maintained apart from these barriers.

There is little need to elaborate these observations. However, it may be useful (because there appear to be important implications that follow) to point up a too little recognized adjunct of the institutionalized separation of the two social psychologies. This has to do with very mundane and practical matters, the sort of thing that few are able to admit into their conscious appreciation of why they believe what they do about their fields or why they proceed as they do in their work.

Again, a conversation will make the point. This conversation, occurring roughly a dozen years ago, was with a young social psychologist, perhaps a year or two out of graduate school. It had to do not with the two social psychologies per se, but rather with the "crisis" in social psychology as defined by Gergen in his influential "Social Psychology as History" (Gergen, 1973) paper. This social psychologist, trained in psychology, accepted Gergen's argument in that paper including the rejection of the experiment as a way of producing sound social psychological information and testing social psychological theory. Why, then, I asked him, did he continue to do and to publish experimental work. His answer was revealing in its directness and its simplicity: he said, "I have to make a living."

Consider the position of an untenured social psychologist in a department of sociology. In terms of specialization, s/he will be in a minority within the department, with the majority interested in social organization: and they will define that interest in contradistinction to social psychology. Thus, our hypothetical young social psychologist in a department of sociology will very likely have to face an intellectual climate which regards what s/he does as not really sociology at all, as--horrors!--psychology (this is particularly true if what s/he does is in the form of laboratory experimentation). S/he is likely to have to be responsive to, and--most importantly and consequentially--to be judged by at least some colleagues who would just as soon rid the department of extraneous elements, meaning those who are defined as not really sociologists at all. S/he is likely to have to deal with reviewers and editors who say in response to what s/he writes: "Where's the sociology?" and is especially likely to have that question raised if individual personality or biological variables are taken to be causal with respect to whatever is under study. In brief, s/he runs very considerable professional risk for doing work that is "contaminated" by psychology, risks in terms of publication, and--independently of publication--risks in terms of salary, promotions and tenure.

Exaggeration? Perhaps. But there is too much truth in the scenario sketched to be ignored. And, there is no reason to believe that anything but details would have to be changed to have the scenario apply to untenured social psychologists in a department of psychology. Indeed, given that such persons are likely to be in a smaller minority, given the biological and physiological foci of much of the field of psychology, given the field's overall focus on individual psychological processes, and given the ideology of science held by many psychologists, any intrusion of a truly social focus in their work is likely to draw even more negative responses than in the situation first described.

Such accounts of the two social psychologies as have been presented raise two obvious questions:

1. Can the kinds of intellectual, organizational, attitudinal and cognitive barriers that keep the two social psychologies separate be changed?

2. What would be the consequence of change such that the barriers between the two no longer existed in any important kind or degree?

Although the second question deserves priority--because only if the cost-benefit equation implicit in the question produced results that indicated that the costs did not outweigh the benefits at an unacceptably high level is the question of the possibility of change worth raising at all--I will begin with the first. And I will answer it using an extreme "no barriers whatsoever" criterion of change in order to make the analysis as forceful as possible.

In my judgment, to effect radical change in the relations of the two social psychologies such that the gap between them could/would disappear is for all practical purposes impossible. The reasons for this judgment are implied in what has already been said.

The source of the gap is clearly institutional. Were institutional separation overcome, differences in intellectual traditions, goals, attitudes, and cognitive biases would disappear in relatively short order, if not in the generation of persons initially entering a new institutional arrangement of common departments in common academic divisions, common publication outlets, common professional organizations and professional meetings, etc., then surely in successive generations of their students. Thus, the question being raised translates into: Can there be developed a framework of institutions that brings together the practitioners of each of the two social psychologies in a way that eliminates fundamental sources of differentiation?

Here, lessons are available from earlier experiments in interdisciplinary experiments that failed, not because people lacked good will or commitment to an interdisciplinary ideal, but because they were slowly but inexorably pulled back into the organizational orbits defined by their respective disciplines. It seems to me that the basic lesson available from those experiments is that unless the new forms of organization--new departments, new journals, new professional organizations--can spring into place instantaneously, and in such a way as to isolate those social psychologists who were trained in departments of psychology from their former colleagues in departments of psychology and those social psychologists trained in departments of sociology from their former colleagues in departments of sociology, they are doomed to failure. Since instantaneous social organizational arrangements are not of this world, extant arrangements will continue to work their effects--and these effects sum to the continuation of the two distinctive social psychologies. Disciplinary loyalties, reinforcing distinctive intellectual traditions, goals, attitudes and cognitions will hold sway, both because that is the way socialization and the reinforcement of social norms in general occurs and because of the social processes implied by the "making a living" story recounted above. As long as the people we talk to, work with, and live with, and as long as those who control our rewards act to implement the specifically disciplinary values of psychology and sociology respectively, the development of a single, ideal "interdiscipline" of social psychology can not occur. And since current arrangements that dictate who we talk to, work and live with, and who controls our rewards cannot be changed literally overnight, they are unlikely to be changed at all in ways that will affect fundamentally the separation of the two social psychologies. Some might object that interdisciplinary experience in the hard sciences--e.g., the emergence of a biochemistry--denies the argument being made. I do not believe that it does, if only because there is and likely always will be less of a problem of scarce resources in the "hard" as compared with the social sciences.

Whether this analysis is a reason for despair depends on the costs and benefits of separating the two social psychologies. I began with an assertion that the general evaluation of the existence of two distinctive social psychologies was negative, i.e., that the focus has been on the costs involved, without commensurate attention to possible benefits. That assertion obviously implies that both costs and benefits exist.

The costs are fairly straightforward, both for each of the two social psychologies and for the possibility of an ideal social psychology: They have to do with the limitations of partial perspectives and the possibility of overcoming those limitations were the conceptions and insights to be derived from each of the social psychologies integrated. They have to do with the strong possibility of theoretical misspecification, failures of understanding that result from the absence of crucial variables in our analyses. They have to do with blind spots arising out of disciplinary myopia. And they have to do with the losses entailed in not taking advantage of the full range of intellectual, theoretical, and methodological resources available on both sides of the social psychological fence.

In addition, and a bit less straightforward, are the kinds of costs entailed in disciplinary-based sniping at one another, both inside and outside of academe, mutual derogation that results in loss of both real and symbolic resources that could be used to the greater glory of a common enterprise (not to speak of the material comfort of individual social psychologists!). My experience on grants committees, for example, is that paradigmatic differences between reviewers and applicants *within* the broader field of social psychology, frequently although not inevitably tied to differences between the two social psychologies, will do more to kill a proposal's prospects for support than will criticism from outside that broader field. Equivalent experience exists with respect to the journal review process. Surely, were there a single institutional framework within which a vision of a common social psychology could develop, such costs could in important degree be avoided. It has also been my experience that, as already suggested, similar sniping takes place inside the academy, with real costs with respect to promotions, tenure, and the development of programs and projects.

Are there indeed benefits to be derived from the continued existence of the separate social psychologies? Suppose my analysis of the near impossibility of effectively integrating the two social psychologies on an institutional level was in error, and that a unified social psychology could realistically be expected to emerge over time if sensible steps were taken now. Should we then press for the immediate formation of an appropriate framework of institutions, inside academe and outside of it, that would facilitate that unification?

My answer to that last question is "no". More completely, my response is "slow down and think carefully about the matter." Think about the potential costs of a merger, both from the standpoint of individual social psychologies and an ideal, single social psychology.

That there would be costs to an integration of the two social psychologies--or, to reverse the imagery, that there are benefits in the continued existence of the two separate social psychologies, disjunctures and all--is on a theoretical level suggested by the long-standing sociological truism that every social arrangement is functional and dysfunctional at the same time, that every social structure has both positive and negative consequences.

Even accepting the correctness of the analysis which argues that, for all practical purposes, the continued existence of the two social psychologies cannot be otherwise, it is not merely pollyannish to assert that some very good things accrue from the separation so frequently deplored. And, understanding that there may well be such benefits can in itself help each of the social psychologies avoid some of the costs of the separation.

There is one benefit of the gap from which, in a sense, all others flow; somewhat paradoxically, this key benefit has a quite particularistic, even "selfish," character. Simply put, it is that sociological social psychology--defined by its foci, key assumptions, approach and attitude--would not survive a thorough-going closure of the gap.

In part, the prediction entailed here issues out of the place of social psychology in most contemporary departments of sociology. As suggested earlier, many so-called structuralists in sociology would gladly be rid of social psychology within departments of sociology, and they would fight the re-emergence of social psychology within their departments were sociological social psychologists to move into other administrative academic units. More importantly, however, within a common institutional framework unaccompanied by the kinds of separate institutional arrangements that now exist, sociological social psychology would be absolutely overwhelmed: The force of numbers virtually guarantees this outcome. The argument, here, assumes that the current rough proportionality that exists in numbers of sociological social psychologist and numbers of psychological social psychologists would be maintained. Given the numbers, the kinds of pressures described earlier as operating within the present structure to keep the social psychologies apart would operate within common institutional settings to homogenize them, and the resultant blend would contain very little sociology. The argument being made also assumes that ideas cannot survive effectively over the long haul the absence of an institutional base, an assumption underwritten by sociology of knowledge and sociology of science evidence that cannot be reviewed here. Surely, ideas are important, "independent" forces in human experience. Just as surely, institutional arrangements can and will either blunt or enhance the power of ideas *per se*. It must be added that there is much beyond sheer numbers that is important to the argument presented, including the ideological attractiveness (at least in the United States) of an individualistic emphasis relative to an emphasis on the social, the likelihood that the former will draw more "external" support than the latter, the ease in translating the former into research product, etc. To forecast a point to be elaborated shortly, the current separate institutional base of sociological social psychology protects against such pressures having the indicated effect within such common institutions as exist now.

The validity of this analysis is evidenced by the experience of editors of what used to be called *Sociometry* and is now called *Social Psychology Quarterly*. Given the numbers of sociologists who do social psychology and psychologists who do social psychology, as well as the styles of work, rates of submitting papers, etc., that accompany that distinction, editors of *Sociometry/SPQ*--a journal explicitly devoted to an interdisciplinary social psychology--have typically had to resort to a more or less explicit quota system to protect its pages from more-or-less total domination by psychology. (It can be added that it is only sponsorship by the American Sociological Association--a protective base in sociology--that legitimates such discrimination. Indeed, it may even require such discrimination: Reviews of the journal's activities in the context of ASA's Publications Committee invariably raise the question of who uses its space and the justification for the apparent "imbalance" in usage.)

The next question is whether the disappearance of a distinctive sociological social psychology would in some way harm psychological social psychology. Or, is the gap between the two social psychologies "good" for the latter as well as the former? There is reason to believe this latter statement is true. As things now stand, each of the social psychologies acts as a goad to the other. While contact between the two may be minimal, and while there may be less knowledge about sociological social psychology on the part of psychological social psychology than the reverse, there is some contact and there is some knowledge. Neither social psychology can afford to totally ignore the other. That implies that neither is likely to completely forget the lessons available from the other; in *some* degree psychologists must remain aware of the reality and the import of social--interactional, institutional, social structural--variables; and in *some* degree sociologists must remain aware that the biology and the psychology of the human being make a difference for specifically social outcomes. For this to occur, however, requires the maintenance of distinctive disciplinary roots, ties and support.

To the degree that the two social psychologies come together on an institutional level, practical exigencies would force curtailment of ties to the parent disciplines of psychology and sociology. Yet, it is the parent discipline of sociology that reinforces, indeed demands, attention to social structure, especially large-scale social structure, just as it is the parent discipline of psychology that reinforces attention to the individual within social psychology as a whole. Further, each part of the whole keeps the other honest, so to speak; each keeps the other from following whatever current intellectual fashion might dictate, whether it be the Marxists' emphasis on the collective or the biologists' emphasis on the genetic. From this point of view, insofar as it is reasonable to talk about progress in social psychology, the progress issues from a process of claim and counterclaim. From this point of view, the movement of social psychology as science is not linear, but dialectic; and the "problem" is to provide institutional support for that dialectic to take place.

Indeed, communication between the two social psychologies is essential; and the communication must be institutionalized in order for it to overcome the real problems envisioned in the usual two social psychologies thesis. Yet, if the argument made in this essay is correct, institutionalized links must occur against a backdrop of institutionalized separation to produce the "creative tension" that is maximally beneficial to social psychology generally. What sorts of mechanisms might provide for both? Panels joining sociologists and psychologists in the discussion of the two social psychologies may be one, although clearly it would be better were the topic underlying the engagements as frequently as possible substantive, i.e., having to do with particular theoretical issues, or particular problems of explanation, or particular assessments of empirical evidence. Perhaps organizations like the Society for Experimental Social Psychology, on the one side, or the Society for the Study of Symbolic Interaction, on the other, might be better utilized to underwrite the desirable dialogue than certainly they are now (SESP generates or accommodates little; SSSI, as far as I know, none at all). *Social Psychology Quarterly* is invaluable in this respect; would that it were joined by its equivalent supported by APA.

To restate the argument by way of concluding this discussion: the two social psychologies need one another, and they need one another in something approximating their current form rather than in a blend of the two. I am not arguing that efforts to bridge the gap between the two social psychologies should be aborted: the dialectic I claim is healthy requires that communication between the two takes place, almost certainly on a level more extensive than is currently accomplished, and that means more forums bringing together representatives of the two social psychologies. Their coming together, however, must be against a context of support from their parent disciplines, and the continued separate disciplinary identification that implies. What we should not be looking towards is a disappearance of the two social psychologies.

Acknowledgements. I appreciate the helpful comments on a draft of this paper by my colleagues, David Heise and Peter Burke.

References

Gergen, K. J. (1973). Social psychology as history. *Journal of Personality and Social Psychology*, *26*, 309-320.

Israel, J., & Tajfel, H. (Eds.) (1972). *The context of social psychology: A critical assessment*. London: Academic Press.

Sewell, W. H. (1989). Some reflections on the golden age of interdisciplinary social psychology. *Annual Review of Sociology*, *15*, 1-16.

Stryker, S. (1977). Developments in "two social psychologies": Toward an appreciation of mutual relevance. *Sociometry*, *40*, 145-160.

8
Is Unity Possible? A Summary

Thomas F. Pettigrew

Introduction

The idea for this volume emerged out of repeated sessions on "social psychological unity" at the annual conventions of both the American Psychological and American Sociological Associations. Indeed, most of the chapter authors have performed at these parallel performances regularly. Large and enthusiastic audiences have generally attended. And in time we came to know each other and our views well.

But were these almost-annual occasions simply preaching to the converted? Was there not a danger that the exercise would degenerate into routine and empty rhetoric? Cookie Stephan decided to act. At her suggestion and prodding, this book took shape with the aim of furthering both wider and deeper discussion of the issues across the emerging discipline. She is truly the originator and senior editor of the volume.

The seven authors are not of one mind. While there is considerable agreement concerning the negative consequences of present arrangements, there are significant differences of opinion concerning the form and benefits of possible remedies. To be sure, these authors have thought and written on the subject more than others. They differ from most social psychologists in that they routinely cross the sub-field boundaries in their own work and read research literatures across the social psychological spectrum. Consequently, the book has an intended bias toward favoring varying degrees of greater communication across the discipline's branches.

There remain, however, significant points of disagreement in the foregoing chapters. Often these differences have been cast in the volume as psychological *versus* sociological perspectives on the field. But, with House, I believe the picture is more complex. Within each of the root disciplines, there are contrasting perspectives as well. Experimental social psychology dominates the psychological wing. But contextual social psychology (called "psychological sociology" by House) has flourished in psychological as well as sociological departments. The names of Donald Campbell, Hadley Cantril, Kenneth Clark, Robert Kahn, Daniel Katz, Herbert Kelman, Theodore Newcomb, and Muzafer Sherif spring to mind. Some famous contextualists, such as the late Herbert Hyman, work in sociology departments but come from psychological backgrounds. Among the present authors, Walter Stephan represents experimental social, and Schooler and I represent contextual social from psychological backgrounds.

Likewise, sociological social psychology is split between contextual social psychologists and symbolic interactionists. Cookie Stephan, House, and Backman represent the former school, Stryker the latter. A fully inclusive view would have also involved additional sociological schools with primarily micro-level interests--in particular, the ethnomethodologists (Garfinkel, 1967; Handel, 1982). It is unfortunate that we were unable to obtain an ethnomethodological commentary for the volume. But it is no surprise that five of the seven contributors are contextual social psychologists, the branch that by definition concerns itself with linking levels of analysis across the discipline.

We must, then, discuss both the negative and positive sides of the unity issue within social psychology in order to summarize adequately the range of views advanced in this book. First, we will consider the negative side of the ledger--that is, the many problems and barriers, both conceptual and practical, that have been discussed throughout the volume. These are the problems that are raised by the field's deep splits as well as the many barriers that perpetuate these splits and make unity difficult. Then, we shall turn to the positive side of the previous chapters--the cited advantages of greater unity and the trends of convergence already evident. Finally, on the basis of these pro's and con's, the chapter closes with possible means for achieving greater intercommunication, with concrete recommendations for realistic, near-term efforts.

Problems and Barriers

This volume has traced and detailed the web of causes for the present disunity of social psychology. As the Stephans make clear in their introduction, social psychology in the United States has two distinct historical origins--one grounded in sociology, the other in psychology. Though William James is a common ancestor and many have crossed the boundary in their individual work, the two historical lines have developed in largely separate streams.

These separate origins, as Schooler emphasizes, meant the two historical lines evolved in sharply different academic environments. Each line, embedded in rival disciplines, developed diverse intellectual traditions. One result, as chapter 3 illustrates, is conflicting meanings for the same basic concepts, such as "secondary analysis" and "norms." More significantly, these different traditions perceived *science* itself differently. The symbolic interactionists, especially the wing formed by Herbert Blumer at Berkeley, adopted a staunch anti-positivistic stance similar to that of Germany's Frankfurt critical school. Experimental social psychologists adopted a modified version of the logical positivism that has long dominated experimental psychology. Indeed, this branch virtually had to emulate psychology's beliefs in order to gain fragile departmental acceptance following World War II (Pettigrew, 1988b). Contextual social psychologists in both root disciplines typically adopt a middle-ground epistemology more suitable for field research.

How fundamental are these differences? Contributors to this volume disagree somewhat on this critical point. Stryker, the lone symbolic interactionist commentator, sees more barriers to unity in general than others. And he appears to perceive the epistemological barriers to be quite formidable. Others disagree.

In my earlier chapter, I argued that these differences are central but not insurmountable. And I advanced Karl Popper's critical rationalism as a promising middle-ground both as epistemology and as a philosophy of science. Critical rationalism, after some softening of Popper's absolutist denial of induction, closely describes the current, unstated, "working" epistemology of the contextual branch. It also approaches the actual practices and assumptions of "post-crisis" experimental social psychology, especially in its Lewinian characteristics. And critical rationalism averts the severe strictures of logical positivism to which symbolic interactionists most object (rightly, in my view). Indeed, the more structural and quantitatively-oriented Iowa-Indiana wing of the school, epitomized by Stryker himself, as well as younger symbolic interactionists of all schools, appear to be shaping a stance far closer to critical rationalism than the Blumer position of earlier generations.

But disparate histories, intellectual traditions, and epistemologies are not the only barriers. These broad differences are furthered by the institutional arrangements and micro-processes that they have set in motion. The fundamental structural problem, as several chapters stress, is the separation across departments. As academics know all too well, departments serve as entrenched academic fiefdoms protected by exaggerated intellectual boundaries. They make intellectual development for all interdisciplinary and interstitial disciplines difficult. Note how interdisciplinary programs suffer most when economic cutbacks hit universities in both North America and Europe.

The effects on social psychology of these rival fiefdoms have been extensive. Both contact and intercommunication across the discipline's various branches have been severely hampered. On several occasions when presenting colloquia, I have had the embarrassing experience of introducing to each other for the first time social psychologists who are on the same large campus but reside in different departments.

Applying the discipline's own insights to this situation, it should come as no surprise that perceived status differentials have arisen. Social psychologists are sometimes second-class citizens in both sociological and psychological departments: not "structural," "macro," and theoretical enough for many other sociologists, not "fundamental," "micro" and positivistic enough for many other psychologists. As Backman pointedly notes, these perceptions can be reflected in less-than-proportional resources for social psychology programs, since the programs can always be regarded as not truly *central* to their root disciplines.

Similar problems of perceived status differentials extend, unfortunately, into the discipline itself. Academic departmental status correlates roughly with the date and circumstances in which departments were established and the size to which they have grown. Psychology departments usually evolved out of deeply-rooted, prestigeful philosophy departments. They came into being on most campuses in North America well before sociology departments, which often evolved from less-rooted, less-prestigeful economics departments. More traditional institutions, such as Amherst and Williams Colleges, have established small sociology departments only within the past generation. Many smaller colleges in the United States still combine sociology with anthropology into one department. Incredibly enough, some universities, such as Washington University in St. Louis, have even disbanded their sociology departments recently.

Size is also a factor. Ever since clinical psychology developed after World War II, psychology departments have grown rapidly in large part because of interest in applied careers in clinical, counseling, and related fields. This growth led to clinicians outnumbering all other psychologists by the 1970s, and the inevitable rupture in the American Psychological Association caused by the conflict between issues of practice and science. Until recently, however, applied sociologists formed only a small part of their discipline. This difference translates into psychological departments being typically much larger than sociological ones on most campuses. This situation, too, lends further campus status to psychology.

This differential status between psychology and sociology departments reflects itself within social psychology in many ways. Backman and Stryker discuss several of these effects. For example, even among American undergraduates interested in social psychology, sociology majors seem far more likely to take psychology courses than psychology majors are to take sociology courses. The typical size difference between the departments usually means that interdisciplinary programs, such as the one Backman has maintained at the University of Nevada at Reno for many years, are likely to be inundated with psychology students. The imbalance of students, and often staff as well, makes it difficult to maintain a truly interdisciplinary approach. In Europe, I find this division even more sharply drawn. With students choosing their field upon entry into university, neither sociology nor psychology students or staff have occasion for joint work. Most of my social psychology students in the Psychology Faculty at the University of Amsterdam literally do not know where the sociology faculty is located--though it is actually only one kilometer or one metro stop away.

But the most troubling effect involves one-way communication. Like Schooler, I came out of a largely psychological background and have long been embarrassed by the near-total ignorance of sociological social psychology by some of my social psychological colleagues in psychology. What makes it especially embarrassing is that most of my social colleagues from sociological backgrounds, Backman, House, and Stryker as prime examples, are so thoroughly acquainted with the relevant social psychological literatures from psychological sources.

Nor is this sharp contrast a limited phenomenon. The one-way communication track is made painfully evident in journal citations. Consider cross-boundary citation data developed for this chapter from recent social psychological journals. Omitting all references to fields other than sociology and psychology, the 1989 issues of *Social Psychology Quarterly* contained 921 citations of which 45.8% were from psychological sources. Compare this generous figure with the tiny percentages of sociological citations in the 1989 issues of the *Personality and Social Psychology Bulletin* (3.5%) and the *Journal of*

Experimental Social Psychology (3.7%). Similarly low percentages hold for the psychological flagship journal, the *Journal of Personality and Social Psychology* (JPSP) during the last half of 1989 (volume 57). Omitting the personality processes and individual differences section, sociological references constituted only 4.1% of the attitudes and social cognition section and 8.0% of the interpersonal relations and group processes section (total=5.9%). These data are not sharply different from the same journals two decades ago (Liska, 1977: p. 5; Segal & Segal, 1972).

Nor is this one-sided communication simply a North American phenomenon. The percentages of sociological citations in the 1989 issues of the *European Journal of Social Psychology* (3.8%) and the *British Journal of Social Psychology* (5.4%) are in the same meager range. Indeed, these small means are deceiving and, if anything, understate the case. Indeed, just one contextual article on aging and susceptibility to attitude change provides 22% of the JPSP's whole volume's references to sociological sources (Krosnick & Alwin, 1989).

The few sociological references that do appear are so patterned and repeated that they starkly reveal the narrow prisms through which the sociological literature is viewed. Hence, the popularly known writings of Erving Goffman, together with those of George Herbert Mead, form the bulk of citations to symbolic interactionism. The majority of articles contain no sociological references whatsoever. Those that do cite a reasonably broad selection of sociological work are generally in areas where the convergence of the branches of social psychology is now clearly recognized--close relationships, stigma theory, etc.

True, some of this huge discrepancy is accounted for by the fact that articles written by psychologists are welcomed in the *Social Psychology Quarterly* while few articles by sociologists appear in the psychologically-oriented journals. But this fact itself vividly documents one-way communication. It is also true that the symbolic interactionist branch is not nearly as open to psychological sources as the contextual branch. Thus, *Symbolic Interaction* in 1987 (volume 10) had a combination of 437 sociological and psychological references, only 5.0% of which are psychological in origin. Finally, these data do not control for the much larger volume of published social psychological research in psychology than in sociology. But even allowing for these qualifications, one-way communication is clearly the dominant norm.

Intergroup conflict theories in social psychology have much to say about such a situation. Here we have groups with similar interests but of unequal size and perceived differential status that have restricted contact and largely one-way communication. These theories would all predict that the usual dismal set of negative symptoms should develop--gross misconceptions of each other, negative outgroup stereotypes, and resistance by both groups to ideas of unity and "integration."

In chapter 3, the Stephans make clear that social psychologists are not exempt from their own theories. The "...goals, methods and theories of each," they write, "are often misunderstood or misrepresented by the other group." From these distortions, negative stereotypes arise on both sides. The Stephans, who uniquely represent both root disciplines within their household, assert that the sociological stereotype capsules experimental social psychologists as "reformed rat runners." Artificial laboratory experiments abound, deceiving college students for 50 minutes. Then experimental social psychologists, according to the stereotype, grossly overgeneralize their findings to society and humankind oblivious to biased sampling and the power of broader social structure outside the laboratory.

In turn, the Stephans tell us that the psychologists' stereotype of contextual social psychologists is that they have only one variable: socio-economic status (SES). And the view of symbolic interactionists is that they are only interested in "nuts and sluts," lose their "objectivity" with their close-at-hand methods, and typically overgeneralize from their single case. Moreover, both sociological groups are thought to be insensitive to individual differences. Schooler adds yet another part of the stereotype that I, too, have often encountered: Namely, that sociologists are not as sophisticated and well trained in statistics as psychologists.

Hopefully, these descriptions are overdrawn. In my own experience, these negative stereotypes are most common among sociologists and psychologists who are *not* themselves social psychologists. They also exist most widely within the discipline among the two branches with the least cross-boundary contact--symbolic interactionists and experimental social psychologists.

Note also two revealing aspects of these dual stereotypes. First, each group criticizes the other in much the same manner that they themselves are criticized within their root disciplines. Second, both stereotypes dwell on the different conceptions among the branches concerning validity. As mentioned in chapter 1, sociological social psychologists typically focus on external validity, so they criticize their psychological counterparts as weak in this regard. Likewise, experimental social psychologists, with their typical focus on internal validity, criticize their sociological counterparts as weak in this manner. Both of these phenomena fit Campbell's (1968; Brewer & Campbell, 1976) contentions concerning stereotypes. The first shows the defensive, motivational functions served by these "scratches on our minds;" the second shows the social comparison, contrast nature of the selected content.

Most social psychologists of all varieties have probably encountered such biased views. Witness how all the chapters of this volume respond to them in part. Of course, there *is* a kernel of truth in each crude portraiture, as there generally is in group stereotypes. But, like most stereotypes, gross ignorance is also involved. They fly in the face of the published data: for instance, that laboratory experimentation accounts for less than half of research by social psychologists in psychology, and various forms of experimentation account for almost a fourth of the research by social psychologists in sociology (Wilson & Schafer, 1978).

With restricted contact and limited communication, these misconceptions are easily maintained by all the many processes that have been uncovered by social psychology itself. For example, I have met several psychological specialists in the social comparison and distributive justice areas who were quite familiar and impressed with the extensive laboratory experimentation in the field by Karen Cook. But they maintained their stereotype of sociologists by simple denial. They simply were unaware that she is a sociological social psychologist who conducts her extensive experimental program in her laboratories located in the Sociology Department at the University of Washington.

Another symptom surfaces in the resistance by some to ideas of unity and "integration." From the larger group, there is the typical denial of any benefits to be had from unity since they question whether sociologists really are social psychologists (e.g., Jones, 1985). For the minority, differential size plays a significant role in arousing fears of being "swamped" by the larger partner--as described vividly by Stryker in his chapter. Consistent, distinctive, "objective" minorities, we know from the research of Moscovici (1985), can be highly influential in changing majorities. But Stryker's principal concern is more akin to ethnic minorities who worry over the loss of their culture. The fear is not so much that sociologically-oriented social psychologists might not be influential in a merged discipline as it is that they might not be able to maintain their distinctiveness.

Indeed, past history is not reassuring on this point. The highly successful joint program in social psychology at the University of Michigan always had a far greater psychological than sociological representation. And its unfortunate destruction was brought about in large part by objections from a few of the sociological participants that the staff and student imbalance led to an unbalanced program.

In sum, then, a formidable array of problems and barriers to closer cooperation within the discipline exists. They include: separate historical origins, intellectual traditions, epistemologies and academic departments; consequent limited intergroup contact and hampered, largely one-way, intercommunication; negative intergroup stereotypes; and differential size with attendant minority fears of being "swamped" if integration were to occur.

What Is There to Be Gained from Greater Unity?

If there are so many barriers, what is there to be gained from greater unity among the discipline's branches? The previous chapters offer an array of answers to this key question. These answers all rest on the validity of a critical set of assertions that can be summarized in three general and interrelated propositions:

1. The various social scientists who call themselves social psychologists share far more than a label. They comprise an emerging discipline with distinctive theory and methods. Thus, *there are numerous similarities between the three main branches of social psychology*: experimental, contextual, and symbolic interaction. In particular, they share a common model of human beings, a common focus on social interaction, and a common, "basic" level of analysis. They even share similar deficiencies--such as the lack of bold theory and a clear conception of levels of analysis. These many similarities, while still largely unrecognized, are causing an increasingly apparent convergence in theory and findings.

2. There are also *critical differences between the three branches*--especially in initial aim, method and epistemology. But, it has been argued, these dissimilarities *tend to be more complementary than conflicting*.

3. Consequently, greater intercommunication would thrive on, rather than be repelled by, both the similarities and the differences among the branches. *Greater intercommunication among the three*, it is argued, *would both broaden and deepen the common enterprise with a powerful triangulation*.

Each of these contentions deserves further comment.

An Emerging Discipline with Important Similarities among the Three Branches

Social psychology is no longer a vague label adopted by disparate social scientists who do not fit into more traditional classifications. Increasingly, the label refers to an emerging discipline. Born from two largely separate roots almost a century ago, social psychology has acquired in recent decades the hallmark of a single intellectual discipline--*distinctiveness*. It now boasts a growing corpus of distinctive theory tested with a variety of distinctive methods. Further, there is now a unique *"social psychology perspective"* that characterizes the new discipline's larger contribution within the spectrum of the social sciences. This perspective, referred to by House as "a meta-theoretical framework" for combining individual and situational properties, differs significantly from those of its parent disciplines.

Such assertions, underlying in varying degrees each of the volume's chapters, necessarily predispose important similarities across the discipline's three principal branches. Social psychology's claims as an emerging discipline, then, rest heavily upon the numerous similarities across its experimental, contextual, and symbolic interactionist divisions. Despite the formidable barriers and limited intercommunication just discussed, these similarities have made themselves more apparent recently through the many convergencies noted in the previous chapters.

In capsule form, consider the following agreements across the branches:

A common model of human beings. Though coming from different parts of the scientific forest, the various sub-fields evince remarkable agreement on a model of human beings. Four general and overlapping terms capture this common model: [1] Bounded rationality, [2] subjectivity, [3] situationally shaped, and [4] reactivity.

> [1] *Bounded rationality*. During the last generation's cognitive revolution throughout psychology, social psychology has moved from a highly rational view of humans toward a middle-ground position. Unlike psychiatry, all the social psychologies view humans not as irrational actors but as reasonably rational creatures within their somewhat restricted cognitive capacities. And, unlike much of economics, the bounded limitations of rationality are also emphasized.

[2] *Subjectivity.* The famous Thomas dictum is cited as central by social psychologists as different as Edward Jones (1965: p. 83) and Sheldon Stryker (Stryker & Gottlieb, 1981: p. 430): "...if men define situations as real, they are real in their consequences" (Thomas & Thomas, 1928: p. 567). Indeed, the field's emphasis on subjectivity, combined with its focus on the situational level of analysis, is what sets social psychology off from the other social sciences. Considering the field's stress on both bounded rationality and subjectivity, it follows that all three branches possess, in their own ways, strong interest in cognition.

[3] *Situationally shaped.* Further, the social psychological model of human beings allows for human beings to be far more malleable in social situations than other models--popular, philosophical, or social scientific. Unitary traits that are immune to situational influences are routinely rejected across the entire discipline. Dramatic experimental demonstrations of the power of situations by Sherif, Asch, Milgram, Zimbardo and Tajfel have impressed experimentalists. Field research demonstrations of patterned similarities across social class, occupational, institutional and other social positions that entail experience in comparable situations, as in the work of Inkeles, Schooler and Kohn, Newcomb and others, have similarly impressed contextualists on this point. Likewise, symbolic interactionists have arrived at the same conclusion from their repeated evidence for patterned reactivity in face-to-face, human interaction.

[4] *Reactivity.* Indeed, the reactivity of human interaction--that actors continuously shape each other in on-going interaction--has won acceptance throughout the discipline. Though long a hallmark of symbolic interactionist thinking, the experimental demonstrations of reactivity by Mark Snyder and his colleagues (e.g., Snyder, Tanke & Berscheid, 1977) has won for it general inclusion in the social psychological model of human beings.

<u>A common focus on social interaction</u>. This common model of human beings has evolved naturally from the common focus of all three branches on social interaction. To be sure, the branches approach this common focus from three directions. Experimentalists typically arrive at their interest in interaction from initial interests at the micro, individual level (Paths B and E in Figure 1 in chapter 1). Consequently, their studies are often criticized by other social psychologists as not being interactive enough, of relying too heavily on

imaginary partners, constraining scripts, initial acquaintances, etc. Contextualists often come from the opposite direction. Their interests in culture and larger social structures frequently lead them to view situations as critically important mediators of macro-level changes leading to micro-level changes in individuals (Paths D and E in Figure 1 of chapter 1). Symbolic interactionists tend to focus initially on the interactional level itself.

A common, "basic" level of analysis and interest in process. These commonalities lead naturally to a "basic" level of analysis for all three branches--the situation. To be sure, many experimentalists work primarily at the micro-level; and some contextualists often work at the macro, structural level. Yet even for these social psychologists, the mid-level of analysis--the situation--is often the end product. Compare, for example, the work of social cognition with that of pure cognitive psychology. Work of the latter is virtually entirely individualistic. Social psychologists who study cognition, however, "socialize" the field with their attention to human stimuli and situational influences--though, perhaps, not as much as other social psychologists might like.

There is an obvious need for social psychology to focus on the interactive, situational level, given the substantive interests of the field. But I believe that there is also a special advantage of working largely at this "basic" level of analysis (Pettigrew & Van de Vijver, in press). Sweepingly global work in the social sciences, from Parsonian theory in sociology to macro-theory in economics, risks too high a level of abstraction to render falsifiable theory. And it can lead to gross examples of the ecological fallacy when applied to individuals. Likewise, sharply narrow, often descriptive micro-level work, from descriptive ethnographies in anthropology to detailed case analyses of psychiatry, risks such a low level of abstraction as not to be generalizable. And when applied to aggregate generalizations, micro-level analyses often commit the compositional fallacy.

The "basic" level of analysis steers a middle course--narrow enough to achieve falsifiable theory and broad enough to generalize. A useful analogy emerges here with the work of Rosch (1973, 1978) on categorization levels. Rosch shows that this middle-range, basic level is the human default level of abstraction. She notes that its principal feature is its intermediate degree of specificity. The basic level, she argues, is common because it is optimal. It is specific enough to be useful and efficient, yet not so specific that it provides more information than necessary. And it is general enough to be used easily, but not so general that it makes too few distinctions. "This is the level at which categories minimize within-category similarity relative to between-category similarity" (Mervis & Rosch, 1981: p. 93). For social psychology, this basic level has also proven to be optimal for studying *process*, another interest in common across the three branches of the discipline.

Common weakness. Not surprisingly, then, the three fields also share some common weaknesses. Two particular deficiencies have been discussed in this volume--the paucity of bold theory in the Popperian sense (chapter 2) and an inadequate conceptualization of levels of analysis (chapter 4). New and specific proposals are advanced in these chapters as promising possibilities for overcoming these general deficiencies. And recent developments, such as Petty and Cacioppo's (1986) elaboration likelihood model, offer hope of a new trend toward broader and falsifiable theory.

Hence, a growing convergence of interests. Considering these many similarities, it is also not surprising that the past few decades have witnessed an increasing convergence of interests across the three branches. A wide range of these convergencies has been mentioned throughout the volume, from labeling, stigma and exchange theories to close relationships, distributive justice and social evaluation. Convergencies are even more apparent in such applied areas as health. More such convergencies can be confidently expected during the 1990s. Yet cross-fertilization even within these common substantive areas of interest has often not been as extensive as one might hope.

Differences between the Branches Are More Complementary than Conflicting

The many similarities and convergencies across the three sub-fields should not blind us to the many differences that remain. Chapter 2 discussed a major such difference--contrasting epistemologies; and it proposed a middle-ground compromise--a modified Popperian approach. Other chapters stressed differences in initial aim and in methods. Yet the basic contention is that these differences are more complementary than conflicting. To be sure, these differences have acted as initial barriers to greater intercommunication; but ultimately, they could serve as advantages in building a broader, deeper discipline of social psychology. The strengths of each field in part, then, address weaknesses in the other two.

In chapter 3, the Stephans emphasize the difference between the various "social psychologies" in their basic aims. I would blunt this argument by rephrasing it as *initial aims*. They are certainly correct that social psychologists based in the two root disciplines face different tasks. Social psychologists in psychology departments are at the *macro*-boundary of their parent discipline. By contrast, those in sociology departments are at the *micro*-boundary of their parent discipline. Each faces pressures to justify their interests in terms of the larger discipline; so psychological social psychologists frequently look downward to the micro-level, while sociological social psychologists look upward to the macro-level.

Thus, for instance, social cognition specialists often feel compelled to demonstrate how their approach contributes to cognitive psychology more generally. And the need for sociological social psychologists, especially contextualists, to justify themselves in macro-level terms is made apparent by many of the introductions they write before introducing their topics to sociological readers. Hence, Rosenberg (1981: p. 592) opens an extended discussion of the self-concept defensively. He admits that it "may strike us as odd" that the self-concept has "sociological relevance;" and that "it may appear to be particularly ill-suited as a subject of sociological concern." Yet it does possess "sociological relevance," he argues persuasively, for the self-concept is both a social product and a social force.

But initial aims and justifications to the root disciplines are one set of concerns; and the final product is often quite another matter. In terms of chapter 2's Figure 1 once again, social psychology in sociology departments often stresses bottom-up analyses (Paths A, B, and C) in order to show the relevance of micro-individual phenomena for the macro-level concerns of sociology. Social psychology in psychology often stresses top-down analyses (Paths D, F, and especially E) in order to show the relevance of macro- and situational phenomena for micro-level phenomena. But there are many exceptions to these trends. Some of the most interesting social psychological research and theory in psychology have been bottom-up in direction. Recall David McClelland's (1961) work on need achievement's role in shaping social structure.

Likewise, in sociological social psychology, micro-phenomena are typically seen, in Rosenberg's terms, as both social products (a top-down process) and social forces (a bottom-up process). Indeed, over the past few decades social psychologists in sociology have taken personality issues far more seriously than those in psychology (Pettigrew, in press). And Rosenberg's (1981; Rosenberg & Simmons, 1972) work on the self-concept and his self-esteem scale are among the most cited and used in this area by psychologists themselves. Moreover, many of the best known contextual studies are almost purely top-down treatments. The Inkeles (1969, Inkeles & Smith, 1974) analysis of modernity's effects on individuals across a variety of cultures, for example, offers a prototype of such top-down analyses. In short, though they seem initially to possess different aims and to face in different directions, social psychology in the two root disciplines ultimately share both bottom-up and top-down perspectives.

As repeatedly noted throughout the volume, the three branches do tend to differ in methods. With their greater concern for internal than external validity, experimentalists prefer the control possible in the laboratory. Symbolic interactionists, maximizing external validity at the possible cost of internal validity, often seek field research and participatory observation. Contextualists typically attempt to balance external and internal validity with such methods as probability surveys. Nonetheless, as we have seen, these differences in method can be easily exaggerated. Increasingly, experimentalists work in the field and sociological social psychologists employ various types of experimental and quasi-experimental designs. Yet to the extent that the three branches bring to the common effort expertise in a wide variety of methods, how can that be anything but positive for a more unified social psychology?

Greater Intercommunication Would Lead to a Promising Triangulation

Greater unity and communication among the three branches of the discipline hold out the bright promise of both methodological and theoretical *triangulation*. Problems could be pursued with a range of methods, samples and settings, from laboratory experiments to field studies and probability surveys. Then problems could determine the method rather than methods shaping the problem. The experimentalists' talent for manipulating variables when possible offers a useful model. Symbolic interactionists bring a sensitivity to the subtle dynamics of interpersonal interaction. Applied to research, their expertise is highly relevant to such phenomena as demand characteristics, evaluation apprehension, and experimental bias (Stryker, 1977). Contextualists offer a wider, probability-driven perspective on the sampling of subjects and situations. Note Schooler's frustration over the general lack of these considerations in experimental social psychology.

On the theory side, the experimentalists typically can provide the most precise intra-individual formulations. The other branches can supply the needed social context at different levels. Symbolic interactionists, with their focus of human interaction, can contribute an inter-individual, situational perspective. And the contextualists can offer a wider, institutional and socialization perspective.

Consider attribution phenomena as a case in point. The various attributional analyses inspired by Fritz Heider's (1958) seminal volume, *The Psychology of Interpersonal Relations*, were advanced by experimental social psychologists and tested in laboratory experiments. Like many theories throughout the discipline, attributional theories center on how human beings subjectively understand the social world. Stryker and Gottleib (1981) point out that Heider shared much with George Herbert Mead. Hence, attribution theory resembles symbolic interactionism in its acceptance of a functionalist, phenomenological, and semi-rationalist perspective.

Yet it is the differences that signal where symbolic interactional ideas and findings can contribute to broadening and deepening attribution theory. The initial attribution formulations in experimental social psychology were individualistic in the extreme, while symbolic interactionists focus on social interaction. Rather than uni-directional causal models about human "biases" and "errors" that assume "objective reality," symbolic interactionism stresses reflexive, reactive, two-way causal models of the negotiated construction of social reality. Thus, it can both methodologically and theoretically "situate" attributional theory. It can do so by focusing on the socially shaped and self-serving "accounts," "disclaimers," and other *socially appropriate* explanations given for norm-breaking behavior. Stryker and Gottlieb (1981: p. 451) pointedly note that attribution theory cannot account for this "sociocultural dependence of *acceptable* explanations." The involvement of self and identity necessarily receive greater emphasis in this interactional approach to attribution--emphases that experimental social psychology itself has increasingly embraced over recent decades.

Contextual social psychologists add to the social context of attribution in a different, more global manner. As its contribution to the triangulation, it typically stresses socialization effects and larger social structural phenomena. For example, Guimond, Begin and Palmer (1989) show in Quebec City that advanced social science university students are far more likely to explain unemployment, poverty and economic disparities with situational and structural, rather than dispositional, attributions than are students in other fields or those beginning their studies in the social sciences. More interesting, these same advanced social science students were also more structural and less dispositional in their explanations than were poor, unemployed youth of the same age. This latter finding violates predictions generated by both the actor-observer and success-failure models of attribution theory. Similarly, other contextual work finds patterned exceptions to the fundamental attribution "error" when subjects account for negative behavior or outcomes of ingroup members or for positive behavior or outcomes of disliked outgroup members (e.g., Guimond & Dube, 1989; Pettigrew, 1979).

Suggested Remedies

The apparent advantages of a more unified social psychology raise the problem of remedy. "It is not enough," House advises, "to simply exhort." So, how do we get there from here? In reply, each chapter has offered remedial proposals at various levels, a few of which are in conflict. Carl Backman, frustrated over the years by the many difficulties of keeping alive a joint social psychology program suspended between sociology and psychology departments, goes furthest. He opts for separate social psychology departments with representation from all branches. Stryker, however, specifically rejects this possibility. He fears being swallowed up by psychology's larger numbers, though this problem could be addressed by ensuring a viable balance between the various branches in any such separate departments.

But there is a larger issue. Social psychology, from its history and content, is a cross-level discipline. Like biochemistry, biophysics and other interstitial fields, it requires easy access to its root disciplines. Separate, isolated social psychological departments would necessarily hinder such needed access. And the well-known, relatively short history of Columbia University's quite separate Department of Social Psychology lends credence to this danger. For this and other reasons, social psychologists of all branches would have reason to be reluctant to adopt Backman's proposal--even if universities were to encourage the development.

In any event, the establishment of new social psychology departments as a widespread phenomenon seems unlikely. Whether a good idea or not, this full-blown model of complete structural integration of the discipline seems not to be part of the foreseeable future. But the unity of the discipline--the focus of this volume--does not depend on the formation of separate departments. The preceding chapters have suggested an array of less sweeping, more viable, and more likely remedies. These proposed means for furthering unity and communication within social psychology center on the gate-keeping nodes of the discipline--(1) graduate training, (2) research institutes, (3) the journals, (4) research funding agencies, and (5) professional organizations and meetings.

1. Graduate training. Social psychologists in sociology and psychology are currently trained in Europe as well as in North America in "splendid isolation" from each other. Little wonder the same concepts come to have conflicting meanings in the separate branches, and negative, exaggerated stereotypes develop of each other. Yet, for House, "it is impossible to be a competent social psychologist without some grounding in both disciplines."

Many of the previous chapters make numerous specific suggestions for alleviating this situation. Most interesting, perhaps, is House's notion of joint work with a problem focus. A product himself of the old joint program at the University of Michigan, House recalls the World War II history of the first emergence of cross-disciplinary work in the field. Wartime demands presented concrete problems to solve with all means available. And this environment, free from the academy's departmental barriers, proved ideal for inducing broad, unified work in social psychology--so much so that Sewell (1989) now looks back on it as "the golden age of interdisciplinary social psychology." This success led directly to the joint programs established at Michigan and Harvard after the war. And it attracted an infusion of young talent into the field whose work became regarded as "classic"--from Samuel Stouffer and William Sewell from sociology to Carl Hovland and Rensis Likert from psychology. House's suggestion is an attempt to use the same means in peacetime to achieve the same unifying effect.

Backman notes an additional plus of dual training. It has been his and my experience that our Ph.D. products who were well-grounded in both root disciplines have the distinct employment advantage of competing in two disciplinary markets.

2. Research institutes. As a countervailing force to increasing specialization, House recommends the establishment of research institutes with a problem focus. Such institutes on university campuses not only can bring all three branches together into a working relationship, but could also serve as a

base for applying generalized graduate training for young social psychologists from both sociological and psychological programs. "...[A]broad and sustained focus on understanding specific social phenomena or problems," House asserts forcefully, "is the *sine qua non* for unifying social psychology."

3. The journals. As Stryker points out, *Social Psychology Quarterly* is the only publication in North America or Europe that welcomes material from all three branches of the discipline. And we have already noted that it is the only social psychological journal with balanced citations. It also boasts an editorial board whose graduate training spans both of the root disciplines. Consequently, several of the chapters recommend strongly that other social psychological journals be encouraged to recruit board members from branches that are currently unrepresented in their pages. Hopefully, this would soon lead to the inclusion of a wider range of articles than is typically true today. Theme issues on topics of mutual interest that span the subfields would advance this process.

4. Research funding agencies. A sensitive and critical gate involves the selection committees of research funding agencies. Frequently, research funding for social psychologists is split between sociology and psychology. This usually means that social psychological funding is competing against proposals from the root disciplines rather than being judged as a body. Eventually, a more unified social psychology will require selection committees with their own line budgets and memberships that are balanced among the subfields. But it would appear that the recommendations at the training, journal, and meeting levels have first priority. My Dutch experience suggests that we will have to become both more informed and tolerant about each other's work before such balanced committees could operate effectively.

5. Professional organizations and meetings. It appears that this area is currently the most ripe for change toward greater intercommunication within the discipline. Social psychologists are in varying degrees alienated from both their parent discipline organizations. Consequently, change is already underway; and these changes could well lead to more focused social psychological organizations that span the subfields without the necessity of relating directly to the parent disciplines.

The Social Psychology Section of the American Sociological Association (ASA) is the basic home of contextualists--though it welcomes and includes members and even officers from all branches. Many in the Section in recent years have become increasingly upset over the ASA's certification program of social psychologists. With understandable concern for the growing unemployment of sociologists during the 1980s, the ASA Council decided the organization should issue certification for various specialties, social psychology among them, aimed at helping sociologists to obtain non-academic jobs. The Social Psychology Section was not consulted about this effort; and a committee was established to do the certifying without Section participation. After strong Section objections, an invitation for one officer of the Section was made to join the committee and then summarily withdrawn. Later one Section representative was asked to serve. To many psychologists, the standards set for certification seemed too minimal. And the attraction for many applicants was to strengthen their chances in seeking *clinical* psychology positions. Apart from the legal and ethical issues raised by this procedure, many contextualists--myself included--lost respect for the ASA in view of the lack of regard the ASA obviously harbored for the integrity and standards of social psychology (Pettigrew, 1986, 1987).

But the ASA conflict is mild compared to the fireworks surrounding the demise of the American Psychological Association (APA) as the umbrella organization of all psychologists. After clinical practitioners used their majority power in the APA to override the interests of psychological scientists, many social psychologists have been prominent in the establishment of a rival organization--the American Psychological Society (APS). This sweeping change has left the three social psychological groups in psychology in a somewhat ambiguous, "wait-and-see" stance. Both the APA's Divisions 8 (Personality and Social Psychology) and 9 (the Society for the Psychological Study of Social Issues--SPSSI) explicitly welcome members who are not members of the APA. Their relationship with the new APS is only now forming. And their future action is complicated by the fact that sizable minorities in both groups are not social psychologists.

The more informal, free-standing, purely social psychological organization, the Society for Experimental Social Psychology (SESP), is prospering in the midst of this flux. And it increasingly spans the interests and membership of both the experimental and contextual branches of social psychology. If the APS does not prove to be an effective home for many social psychologists in psychology, SESP could form the basis of an organization to which social psychologists of at least two branches could base their primary identifications. This joint organizational base would represent a major step toward both greater intercommunication and "social identity" for a more unified discipline.

But increased organizational communication across the branches need not await such structural developments. Special cross-branch study groups and meetings, centering on topics of common interest--stigma, labeling, social networks, the self, identity, roles, close relationships, self-presentation, etc. could be created. They could exploit House's point about the importance of a problem-orientation with programs on such joint applied areas as health, law, gender, aging, and intergroup relations. Invited sessions at various meetings for members of another branch could go beyond the generalized sessions on disciplinary unity that have characterized such meetings of the past decade. Pertinent possibilities come readily to mind: Symbolic interactionists on reactivity at the SESP; close relationship specialists in experimental at the Society for the Study of Symbolic Interaction meetings; contextualists on the institutional bases of social psychological applications at Division 8 meetings.

Summing up, then, greater intercommunication among the branches of the emerging discipline is urgently needed. Stryker, in his chapter, is so optimistic as to believe that this process is inevitable. "Neither social psychology can afford to totally ignore the other," he writes. So "each of the social psychologies acts as a goad to the other." But in the past many social psychologists have *in fact* totally ignored other branches. In any event, in the future the process could be importantly furthered by an array of key structural arrangements involving graduate training, research institutes, journal policy, the actions of research funding agencies, and professional organizations and meetings.

References

Brewer, M. B., & Campbell, D. T. (1976). *Ethnocentrism and intergroup attitudes: East African evidence*. New York: Halsted Press, 1976.

Campbell, D. T. (1967). Stereotypes and the perception of group differences. *American Psychologist, 22*, 817-829.

Garfinkel, H. (1967). *Studies in ethnomethodology*. Englewood Cliffs, NJ: Prentice-Hall.

Guimond, S., Begin, G., & Palmer, D. L. (1989). Education and causal attributions: The development of "person-blame" and "system-blame" ideology. *Social Psychology Quarterly, 52*, 126-140.

Guimond, S., & Dube, L. (1989). La representation des causes de l'inferiorite economique des Quebecois Francophones. *Canadian Journal of Behavioral Science, 21*, 28-39.

Handel, W. (1982). *Ethnomethodology: How people make sense*. Englewood Cliffs, NJ: Prentice-Hall.

Heider, F. (1958). *The psychology of interpersonal relations*. New York: Wiley.

Inkeles, A. (1969). Making men modern: On the causes and consequences of individual change in six developing countries. *American Journal of Sociology, 75*, 208-225.

Inkeles, A., & Smith, D. (1974). *Becoming modern: Individual change in six developing countries*. Cambridge, MA: Harvard University Press.

Jones, E. E. (1985). Major developments in social psychology during the past five decades. In G. Lindzey & E. Aronson (Eds.), *Handbook of social psychology* (3rd ed.) (Vol. 1). New York: Random House.

Krosnick, J. A., & Alwin, D. F. (1989). Aging and susceptibility to attitude change. *Journal of Personality and Social Psychology, 57*, 416-425.

Liska, A. E. (1977). The dissipation of sociological social psychology. *American Sociologist, 12*, 2-8.

McClelland, D. C. (1961). *The achieving society*. Princeton, NJ: Van Nostrand.

Mervis, C. B., & Rosch, E. (1981). Categorization of natural objects. *Annual Review of Psychology, 32*, 89-115.

Moscovici, S. (1985). Social influence and conformity. In G. Lindzey & E. Aronson (Eds.), *Handbook of social psychology* (3rd ed.) (Vol. 2). New York: Random House.

Pettigrew, T. F. (1979). The ultimate attribution error: Extending Allport's cognitive analysis of prejudice. *Personality and Social Psychology Bulletin, 5*, 461-476.

Pettigrew, T. F. (1986). President's message: An issue for section discussion. *Newsletter of the Social Psychology Section of the American Sociological Association, 12 (2)*, 2-4.

Pettigrew, T. F. (1987). *Annual report of the Social Psychology Section. Footnotes (of the American Sociological Association, 15 (4)*, 13-14.

Pettigrew, T. F. (1988). Influencing policy with social psychology. (The 1987 Kurt Lewin Memorial Address.) *Journal of Social Issues, 44 (2)*, 205-219.

Pettigrew, T. F. (In press). Personality and social structure: Social psychological contributions. In S. Briggs, R. Hogan, and W. Jones (Eds.), *The handbook of personality psychology*.

Pettigrew, T. F., & Van de Vijver, F. (In press). Thinking both bigger and smaller: Finding the basic level for cross-cultural psychology. In *European perspectives in psychology*. London: Wiley.

Petty, R. E., & Cacioppo, J. T. (1986) The elaboration likelihood model of persuasion. In L. Berkowitz (Ed.), *Advances in experimental social psychology*. (Vol. 19). New York: Academic Press.

Rosch, E. (1973). Natural categories. *Cognitive psychology, 4*, 328-350.

Rosch, E. (1978). Principals of categorization. In E. Rosch & B. L. Lloyd (Eds.), *Cognition and categorization*. Hillsdale, NJ: Erlbaum.

Rosenberg, M. (1981). The self-concept: Social product and social force. In M. Rosenberg & R. Turner (Eds.), *Social psychology: Sociological perspectives*. New York: Basic Books.

Rosenberg, M., & Simmons, R. G. (1972). *Black and white self-esteem: The urban school child*. Washington, DC: American Sociological Association.

Sewell, W. H. (1989). Some reflections on the golden age of interdisciplinary social psychology. *Social Psychology Quarterly, 52*, 88-97.

Segal, D. R., & Segal, M. W. (1972). How sociological is social psychology? *American Sociologist, 7*, 15.

Snyder, M., Tanke, E., & Berscheid, E. (1977). Social perception and interpersonal behavior: On the self-fulfilling nature of social stereotypes. *Journal of Personality and Social Psychology, 35*, 656-666.

Stryker, S. (1977). Developments in "two social psychologies": Toward an appreciation of mutual relevance. *Sociometry, 40*, 145-160.

Stryker, S., & Gottlieb, A. (1981). Attribution theory and symbolic interactionism: A comparison. In J. H. Harvey, W. Ickes, & R. F. Kidd (Eds.), *New directions in attribution research* (Vol. 3). Hillsdale, NJ: Erlbaum.

Thomas, W. I., & Thomas, D. S. (1928). *The child in America*. New York: Knopf.

Wilson, D. W., & Schafer. R. B. (1978). Is social psychology interdisciplinary? *Personality and Social Psychology Bulletin, 4*, 548-552.